Nice to see you ...

The Bruce Forsyth Story

Nice to see you ...
The Bruce Forsyth Story

STEPHANIE PINTER

FORTI NIHIL DIFFICILE
Northern & Shell Plc

This book first published in 2008 by
Northern & Shell
The Northern & Shell Building
10 Lower Thames Street
London EC3R 6EN

ISBN-13: 978-0-85079-361-1

Internal design and typesetting by Andrew Barker
Cover design by Richard Green
Printed and bound in Italy by Rotolito Lombarda.

Contents

Didn't He Do Well?

THE VENUE WAS London's Dorchester Hotel. The date: 22 February 2008. The cream of Britain's show business establishment was in attendance: guests at the forthcoming party included Dame Shirley Bassey, Ronnie Corbett, Michael Parkinson, Rolf Harris, and Jules Holland. There was to be an informal lunch, followed by a dinner dance at which the birthday boy vowed to dance the night away.

Finally, the host appeared. Typically – and appropriately, given his romantic history – he had a beauty queen on each arm: Miss Puerto Rico, Jennifer Guevara, on his right, and Miss England, Georgia Horsley, on his left. A former Miss Puerto Rico, Wilnelia Merced, was also present, not least because she had been married to the host for twenty-nine years. Basking in the centre of all this attention was the man who was celebrating his eightieth birthday, almost a lifetime in show business, and his status as one of the best-loved entertainers in the country: Bruce Forsyth.

Bruce was dapper as ever and on sparkling form, striking his trademark pose – a cross between a strongman and a thinker. Was he even thinking of retiring? 'I am not that doddery,' he said to the throng of journalists in attendance at the event, and that much was clearly true. 'You try to do live television for two hours on a Saturday night without making a mistake. If I make a fluff, I try to get out of it and say something funny. It's only one a show. I am not doddery. Senile, yes. But not doddery. Adrenalin is a marvellous thing. Whenever I do a show for two hours, afterwards I am still in that frame of mind. Then I start to fade and go downhill and then I have to shut the eyes.'

The show he was referring to was *Strictly Come Dancing*, the latest in a huge series of television triumphs for Bruce, the first of which was a full half-century earlier, when he was catapulted to stardom as the host of *Sunday Night at the London Palladium*. Since then, there have been countless more, the most famous being *The Generation Game*, *Play Your Cards Right*, and *The Price is Right*. When asked why this latest show was so popular, both with the public and its host, Bruce stated,

'It suits me as a show, because I know it goes to people young and old,' said Bruce. 'It is basically a family show, which we have very little of in this country. I have had enough of reality. I want to see performers performing.'

So did the nation, and in Bruce they certainly got that. A consummate professional, Bruce's lifelong work as a dancer certainly kept him in the kind of shape a man twenty years his junior would have been proud of – but then, so would his series of wives. Bruce has had three wives, and six children. His third wife, Wilnelia, a full thirty-two years his junior, is also credited with keeping him in shape: 'We won't talk about the age gap, that will make me feel tired,' he said jovially. 'But she does keep me young. She's the most wonderful lady who has a career of her own. She's been at the forefront of keeping me young. I also have seven grandchildren and two great-grandchildren. If that doesn't keep you going, what can?'

Bruce is, of course, adored these days, not just by the public – who never forsook him even when television, briefly, did – but by his peers in the industry. 'I'm mad about him. He is one of the great performers of our generation – of any generation,' said Greg Dyke, erstwhile director general of the BBC. 'He's got the look, he's got the style, he can do it all. He is a star. You might ask how – or even why – but when you see it you cannot deny it.'

Peter Jackson, head of entertainment at ITV, and Bruce's producer on *The Generation Game*, is similarly enamored. 'He is fabulous,' he said. 'He is a true consummate professional, one of a dying breed of great old-fashioned showmen. I'd rank him with Des O'Connor and Ronnie Corbett – although they're both considerably younger: fantastic entertainers, veterans, not relics, who take us back to the glory days of variety. It was both an honour and an education to work with him on *The Generation Game*. He's done the hard yards, he learned his trade; he can sing, he can dance, he can make jokes, his timing is immaculate. He's one of the very few British entertainers who could take his place beside somebody like Sammy Davis Junior, and match him step for step.'

It's been an extraordinary career and *Strictly Come Dancing* is a fitting last act (if that's what it turns out to be). Bruce himself realises quite what a boon it has turned out to be. 'It sounded fantastic, but I thought it would be more of a comedy show, with the celebrities making mistakes and tripping over their frocks,' he said a couple of days before his birthday. 'I thought it would be more like *Dancing On Ice*! Then I saw the time everyone had been practising, even before we'd started filming, and then the improvement after the first couple of weeks. I saw everyone's competitive streak kick in and I thought, "This is a different show". I'll be back for another series. One thing I've learned over the years is that you never walk away from a hit show, at least not this early on. *Strictly* is still in its infancy. I love the buzz.'

Even so, the show takes its toll, as Bruce has admitted. 'After the live Saturday show I spend Sunday in bed,' he said. 'I get up for breakfast, go back to bed, get up for lunch, watch the football and then back to bed, dinner, and then bed. It's twenty-four hours, more or less, of complete relaxation. That show takes it all out of me – what people don't realise is that I probably make thirty entrances and exits. I have to keep dashing on and off. This is why people say I fluff my lines a bit, but I defy anybody on live TV not to. I had to stop doing jokes where I get a person's name wrong on purpose to get a laugh because people thought I was just getting stuff wrong.'

Contrary to public belief, however, Bruce is not determined to soldier on, come what may. He's as aware as anyone that there is life after show business, and, indeed, his schedule is nothing like what it once was. 'Show business is in my blood, but I take so much time off – I'm

not like other people that have to be "on" all the time,'
he said. 'If I become past it, if I've gone over the top, I
think I'll know. If I don't, then I'll rely on my agent, my
manager, and my wife to tell me it's time to turn in. I
don't feel any different – what are you supposed to feel
like at eighty?'

Indeed, the couple spend a good deal of time in
Wilnelia's native Puerto Rico, which is where they
planned to return to after Bruce's birthday celebrations.
'We'll go back to Puerto Rico and I'll do nothing. I'll read
a few books, go to the beach, eat, and play my golf,' said
Bruce. 'I love it. So, when the time comes for me to give
it all up – and it will be sooner rather than later – that will
stand me in good stead. I won't be pining to be in front
of a camera. We have a lovely home life; I'm much more
relaxed than people think. That idiot who runs on and off
set? I put him to bed on Saturday, and he only appears
the next Saturday when I'm running around like some
frantic insect again.'

'I always say it took me a long time to find the love of
my life, but it was definitely worth the wait,' said Bruce.
'I haven't worked more than six months a year for about
twenty years now, and that's because I love spending time
with my wife. When I met her, I looked at my life in a

completely different way. I can't believe we've been married for twenty-five years; it seems like twenty-five minutes. When we had our wedding anniversary last month, I was sitting quietly thinking, "How can I be eighty?" Then I realised it was also the anniversary of when I started *Sunday Night at the London Palladium*. I can't believe any of it was possible.'

But it was. Bruce has come a very long way since starting out, aged fourteen, as Boy Bruce, the Mighty Atom. For fifty years, Bruce Forsyth has been one of Britain's foremost entertainers. Hasn't he done well?

The Forsyth Saga

IT WAS A warm day in August 1914. The shadow of war was already hanging over Europe, but in Edmonton, north London, all was good cheer. John Thomas Forsyth-Johnson, a twenty-two-year-old cycle and motor mechanic, was about to marry Florence Ada Pocknell. The two of them had no particularly big visions for the future: they had met at the Salvation Army, and wanted nothing more than a happy life together, blessed with children. There was no hint back then that their youngest child was going to become a leading light in show business and one of the best-loved entertainers in the country – indeed, if anyone had suggested such a thing to John and Florence, the two would have scoffed.

Florence was a Londoner, born and bred. She was born in 1894, and her family came from Docklands, where her father, William Robert Pocknell, worked on the 'lighters' – flat-bottomed barges used to ferry goods from one dock to another. The Pocknells were good, working-class stock, and had lived for decades in Bermondsey (now a highly fashionable area, but back then a byword for poverty and neglect). The newly-married couple, however, were to make their way slightly further out of the city centre, to the suburb of Edmonton, where they were to remain for the rest of their married lives.

Bruce's father John, also a native Londoner, came from a slightly more unusual background. His father, Joseph Forsyth-Johnson, was a landscape gardener who married a woman – eight years his elder – who was the daughter of a groom working for the local gentry. They married in 1861, and John was born nine months later in Gilling, Yorkshire. Joseph's grandfather, a Scot who was also called John, was the son of William Forsyth.

William was born in Aberdeen in 1737, developed a deep interest in horticulture, and became a gardener at Syon Park, west London. From there, he went on to be appointed superintendent of the Chelsea Physic Gardens in 1771, and three years after that was put in charge of the grounds at Kensington Palace and St James's Palace. Indeed, such a notable man in his profession was he that not only did he go on to become one of the four founders of the Royal Horticultural Society in 1804, but also a whole genus of plants was named after him. This was, of course, the forsythia. It was from this stock that Bruce was born.

The Forsyth-Johnson's first child was a daughter, Maisie, followed by their first son, John. Five years after John's birth and ten years after Maisie, Bruce came along, on 22 February 1928. The family doted on him from the start. 'I was the baby of the family. I was called Bru or Boo Boo,' he recalled. 'I had such wonderful parents; they were very good people. They both belonged to the Salvation Army; in fact, that's where they met. My father played the euphonium and the cornet and on a Sunday morning, my mother used to sing all the lovely hymns on Edmonton Green, and people would stop and listen to her because she had such a beautiful voice.'

Although Bruce's background was Salvation Army rather than showbiz, all the showbiz elements were there. John played brass instruments, thus inculcating a love of music and rhythm into his son from the outset, while Florence was an excellent singer and seamstress, a talent that came in useful when she was able to run up Bruce's stage costumes in later life. Above all, though, the two were determined that Bruce would follow his dreams. They were not the sorts of parents to discourage him from following a career in show business: rather, they supported him and urged him on right from the very start. Bruce made his stage debut at the age of three, in the local pantomime, singing 'I Lift Up My Finger And Say Tweet Tweet', a performance that brought down the house. From that moment onwards, his fate was assured. Both parents realised that their son was destined for a career in show business, and both could not have been more positive.

While John and Florence certainly were not rich, their children grew up in relative comfort – or as much as could be afforded until the war began. 'We were never terribly well off by any means, but we didn't want for anything,' said Bruce. 'We had a television and a car and every August we used to go down to the lovely beaches in Cornwall. My father worked so hard to keep us at a certain level. He was a garage proprietor; he had a little garage by the side of our house in Victoria Road in Edmonton. He started off with one petrol pump, then he graduated up to two pumps, and in the end he had three petrol pumps. He had some lock-up garages and a little taxi service as well.' He also had a fierce work ethic that he passed on to his youngest son.

Bruce and his brother John were different right from the start. John seemed destined to follow his father into a mechanical trade, while Bruce knew that wasn't what he wanted. His parents seemed to sense it, too. 'You don't want to end up with hands like these,' his father would tell him, holding up hands that were ingrained with dirt – and he was right. 'My head was always up in the air, show business, becoming a big star – that was the only thing I thought about,' Bruce later recalled.

At the time, though, he was irritated. 'John went into my father's garage business,' he recalled. 'He was very interested in engines and he was a good mechanic. I can still see him working down there and getting his hands dirty. My father would never allow me down there. If I went into the garage, he would say, "No, you're not going to get your hands filthy like us", because when you are a mechanic for years and years, that dirt eventually grimes into the hands, and there's no way you can wash it off. I didn't like being told that, because as a kid, you love to get among all the dirt and grease. But I was grateful afterwards, because I could see it protected my hands, and with me playing piano so much, I'm sure it helped that I didn't get my hands all stiffened up.'

To be born in 1928 was to be born in the shadow of the two great wars, but Bruce believed that he was extremely fortunate to have come along when he did. 'I was born at just the right time,' he said. 'A little earlier and I could have been killed in the war, as my brother was. Much later, and I would have missed those golden years, when television was young and exciting.' And to be born to those parents, who were so determined that he should go where fate beckoned, was even better.

Bruce had been hoofing it up from infanthood, but he started to learn his trade in earnest when he began to tap dance. And that tap dancing came about because, when he was eight, Bruce had an experience that was to change his life: he saw Fred Astaire. From that moment on, Bruce knew he wanted to dance. 'As soon as I got home from school, I'd take the carpet up, because there was lino underneath, and I'd tap away,' Bruce later recalled. 'My first dancing teacher was in Tottenham: Tilly Vernon. She couldn't be anything else with a name like that! But she didn't last. I started going to a teacher in Brixton, a journey of two-and-a-half hours each way. My mother would take me. They couldn't really afford the lessons either. We weren't well off. But they were so encouraging.' It was a remarkable stance for his parents to take.

The influence of Fred Astaire cannot be under-estimated: it was something Bruce referred to frequently throughout his career. Asked by an interviewer in the mid-1970s about the early days, he brought it up again. 'I don't know what it was about dancing,' he said. 'But I adored it. Fred Astaire was my hero. I saw all his films at least three times. I loved football, too – anything to do with the feet. Funny, isn't it? I suppose the rest of my body must have been lazy and my feet made up for it. I got into some scraps because of it. I'd be walking home from school, my tap shoes in my hand, and someone would shout, "What have you got there, you big sissy?" It taught you to look after yourself.'

That was playing it down. On another occasion he re-called this in slightly more detail. 'I'd come home from playing football at school, with my boots tied around my neck,' he said. 'I'd have a quick wash, get my tap dancing shoes and my little case, then I'd go off to my dancing lesson. There was one boy down our street who was al-ways calling me a sissy. I got off my bike once and gave him a right pasting.' Physical violence aside, it was a good preparation for the early years: nothing was going to come easily to Bruce. He was going to have to fight all the way.

From early on, Bruce entered dancing competitions, but he encountered problems even there. 'Not many little boys went in for dancing in those days, so I had to use the little girls' changing room,' Bruce related. 'Very embarrassed I was, and my mother used to hold out her coat while I changed.' But he did it, persevered, and each time got that little bit better. He learned that a career in show business was often going to throw up problems in its wake, problems that could only be overcome if he put his heart and soul into it. The ridicule incurred by using the girls' changing room was nothing compared to what he would face as he steadily built up his career.

But John and Florence urged him on: indeed, both parents were extremely encouraging. 'It got a bit embarrassing at times,' Bruce recalled. 'We'd be sitting in the Empire, and whenever a tap dancer came on, my dad would say in a loud whisper, "You're twice as good as him, Brucey. You could eat him for breakfast". I squirmed in my seat: "Sssh, dad, he'll hear you", I would say. But it made no difference.'

It was to take Bruce the best part of two decades in show business before he finally made his name, though he started very young. In 1939, war broke out; it was also the year that Bruce made his television debut. Although the exact details have been lost in the mists of time, the debut was probably on a talent show called *Come and be Televised*, introduced by Jasmine Bligh, which was broadcast from Radiolympia. Bruce and his parents also contributed to the war effort, joining an amateur theatre company in Edmonton and giving shows for charities including the Aid to Russia Fund, the Buy a Spitfire campaign, and many more.

Bruce was typical of a generation of London children who lived during the war. 'I was eleven years of age when war was declared,' he recalled. 'From the moment the war started, the only thing John wanted to do was fight for his country, and the day he turned eighteen he joined up. My life was wrapped up in the war. I'd spend all my time outside of school watching the dogfights. They were quite amazing – looking up in the sky you'd see the vapour from the back of the planes swooping in and out, and you could actually see the bombs raining down from the German planes. Along with the other kids, I would collect shrapnel from all the bombs that had been dropped in our neighbourhood, and if you found a piece with some numbers on it, that's a real keeper's piece. When you're that age, war is romantic. You don't really think how terrible it is.'

Around this same time, Bruce became something of an entrepreneur. 'When I was thirteen, I cashed in on my dancing lessons and opened my own school,' he said in an interview in 1959. 'It was a shilling a lesson in a studio that was part of one of my father's garages. Before long, I had a fair old troupe of boys and girls and enough shillings to make our gas meter man suspicious. We used to do these charity shows to help the war effort.'

It was as far back as this that Bruce began to learn the skill that was to set him head and shoulders above the rest: how to work an audience. It started almost by accident. 'It began when I was the little boy performer,' he said. 'Invariably, the pianist would go wrong with the tempos. So, I would think nothing of stopping in the middle of the routine and going over to this lady with the funny hat – they always wore funny little straw hats – and saying, "No dear, no dear. I want it to be faster. Can you do that?" The audience would start to ripple and that was how it started.'

In 1942, aged just fourteen, he left school. Academia was never going to compare to show business. His headmaster was rather concerned about Bruce's leaving report. 'Don't you worry about a thing, sir,' Bruce told him kindly. 'I'm going into a profession where it's what you do that counts.'

And so Bruce launched himself, with an advertisement

in *The Stage* newspaper announcing that Bruce Forsyth Esq. was 'Vacant for Everything', dropping the 'Johnson' in his surname, as it was too cumbersome. He was to spend the next few years touring up and down the country under the slightly alarming title of Boy Bruce, the Mighty Atom. With war raging, and so many of the able-bodied men away, theatres – and there were still a few open in every city – were crying out for male talent, whatever the age. 'It was easy to get work, so that's how I got into the business,' he later recalled. Bruce's debut was at the Theatre Royal in Bilston starring the Great Marzo at the top of the bill, and the Mighty Atom at the bottom. Bruce played the ukulele and accordion, and tap-danced, in an act that he himself admitted was awful. 'My first professional job, at Bilston, was nearly my last,' he later recalled. 'The show folded up after a week. I began to realise the kind of life I'd chosen. One week in a job; the next week out.' Nor had it been a financial success: Bruce's share of the profits was just 13s 4d. 'I had to send home to my parents for money for my lodgings and my train fare home, so my first week in show business cost them about £3,' he said wryly, many years after the event.

In 1943, however, tragedy struck. Bruce's older brother John was an RAF pilot and was posted missing.

His body was never found; he was almost certainly killed during a training mission in Scotland. On the day his brother died, Bruce had a strange, near out-of-body experience. He had been touring English air bases, entertaining American servicemen. While playing cricket, he hurt his hand and was sent to lie down. He fell asleep. 'I had this curious feeling I was in an aeroplane,' he recalled. 'I was over the sea and had to get out, had to jump. As I jumped, I woke up, and had to stop myself falling onto the floor.'

When he returned home a few days later, Bruce was told that his brother was lost at sea during a training exercise at Turnberry (he later discovered John had gone missing searching for survivors of a training accident). 'It was a house that had a very warm atmosphere, and it was suddenly cold. It was very weird,' he said of being back at home. John's body was never found. 'To be posted missing is the worst of all,' said Bruce. 'My mother, particularly, went on for weeks, months, even years saying, "Oh, he could have been picked up by a steamer ... maybe he's lost his memory and one day he'll be back."'

It was a terrible tragedy that struck at the heart of what had been a very happy childhood. 'One day my parents said they were going up to Turnberry, because they'd never been to the area, and I went with them,' Bruce later recalled. 'I'd been called up myself by then: I was in the RAF. It was a very sad pilgrimage, and when we got there we didn't know where to look or what to do. All we could do was just take in the fact he was lost there. And then I had to get back to my base, and I was very upset to leave them that night; I wanted to be with them and see if I could comfort or help in any way, because my mother was very upset.'

Many years later, Bruce was asked if the weight of parental expectation had shifted to him: 'I never felt that,' said Bruce. 'But it destroyed the whole family for a while. He was posted missing, and for years afterwards my mother still thought there was a chance he'd been picked up by a boat somewhere and had been taken to South America. But I didn't feel any pressure. Show business was all I wanted to do, anyway.'

During the war, Bruce worked for the Red Cross, doing song and dance acts at American army camps all over the country. And while it might have been a hard life, it was also wildly exciting for a fifteen-year-old boy. 'How well we were treated!' Bruce recalled. 'I remember going into a top Manchester hotel and being shown into a room with a telephone. What luxury for a fifteen-year-old. I immediately phoned home and said this was the life for me. And so it was for the next four years.'

It was during the war, when he was fifteen, that he had his first great romance, with another fifteen-year-old, Irene Wilson. Many, many years later, he was shocked to hear that she had died in a house fire at the age of seventy-seven. 'I am deeply shocked and saddened. Irene was a terrific woman. I've got many happy memories of our time together,' declared Forsyth, then also seventy-seven, to the *Daily Express*. 'The very strange thing is that I was thinking about Irene on the Monday [the day she died]. I thought it was about time I wrote to her, as we hadn't spoken in years. Irene was a great singer in the big bands of the Fifties and Sixties. We met during the war in a show. I was playing the piano for all the acts. As the German bombs fell on London, we entertained members of the public to try to keep up their morale. We quickly became very close and I used to visit her and her family regularly.'

'I would travel to the family home in Sydenham and play the piano and she would sing. They were fantastic, fun times. Irene was good for a laugh. She was always so happy. She had an amazing sense of humour, and I always thought that if she hadn't made it as a singer, she would have been doing stand-up comedy. She had a great singing voice and used to tour the country doing shows. This is a sad day for me. This is a huge tragedy. She was a lovely woman.'

Despite the excitement of his first romance, Bruce's main ambition at that time was to get into theatres owned by Moss Empires, which he eventually did. 'They were a different thing altogether,' he said. 'The dressing rooms were better, the bands were better, the stage door was clean, and when you looked out, the seats were a nice plush rather than all worn and dirty. And there were boxes!'

So began sixteen years' slog in an effort to break into the big time. It was not easy, but it was to prove a valuable experience later on, not least when Bruce finally got his big break with *Sunday Night at the London Palladium*, something he himself was very aware of. 'I did second-spot comedy in variety; it was the most terrible spot you could have,' he said years later. 'Before I got the *Palladium* job, I did four years of concert party sketches. So when I came to the Palladium I had no problem taking over "Beat the Clock", the game that we had in the show.'

His life was very different from the luxurious exis-tence it became: at one stage, he was touring round the country in an old Wolsey with a caravan attached to it. An easy life it was not. Sounding uncharacteristically sour, he said, 'I was the second-spot comic, which is the hardest job in the world, the lowest form of animal life in show business. I had a terrible time at the Empress in Brixton. I don't know what it is now. I hope it's a bingo hall. I hated the place.'

Right from the start, Bruce knew what he wanted to be: a family entertainer, strictly middle of the road. Even in the late 1950s, just before he got his big break, Bruce knew exactly the type of performer he wanted to be. 'When Elvis came along, I became an angry young man, but for different reasons to everyone else,' he explained in a rather telling interview when he was in his seventies. 'I became angry because all these songs, which had three chords in them, suddenly usurped the music of my youth.' His favourites were Oscar Peterson and Bill Evans: 'I don't care what you're into. If you're a musician, you should really hear how those pianists approach their instrument. The most important notes are the ones they leave out.'

Bruce's early years toughened him up. 'One trip I remember was from Barry Docks in Wales to Sunderland,' he recalled. 'It took eighteen hours in those days – no motorway, you see. I arrived at the digs, completely whacked out, asleep on my feet. I knocked at the door and the landlady sort of leaped out at me. "Supper's ready," she said. And there on the plate was the most minute pork pie you have ever seen and about twelve peas. I was too tired to argue and went straight to bed. I hardly got a wink of sleep – the bed was too small. I got up in the night and discovered that at the foot of the bed was an empty beer crate to make it bigger. In the morning, I complained. "I can't understand it," the landlady said, getting on her high horse. "The last gentleman thought the bed was wonderful". Well, I made some inquiries and it turned out that the "last gentleman" was one of a troupe of circus midgets.'

Even the times Bruce looked forward to often went wrong. 'In the early days, I was booked to play at the Wood Green Empire in London, the theatre where I used to go with my parents as a boy,' he recalled. 'I got so excited about it. At last, I thought, I'm appearing in front of my own people. They will love me; there will be this great affection between us. Some homecoming! I'd only been on a few seconds when someone threw fish and chips at me.'

This actually upset Bruce a good deal, but he recovered almost immediately. 'I did get a joke out of it: I walked over and opened them and – the audience didn't know whether to laugh or what – I just got one of the chips and put it in my mouth and said, "No salt and vinegar? For goodness sake, what class have you got?" And the audience was on my side.'

Hurtful as it might have been at the time, it was building Bruce up into the entertainer he was to become. Not only did it toughen him up and turn him into the consummate professional – to this day, although he can be exacting, it is impossible to find anyone who would say that Bruce is difficult to work with – but it also provided the material he was going to be able to put to good use for years ahead.

Most importantly, it taught him how to handle an audience. Bruce can be very rude to those who come to see him – 'I see I've at last reached your level … and believe me, it's been downhill all the way' is one typical rejoinder – but he never insults them or goes too far. He's not just performing for them: he's actually one of them. (It was this talent that was put to particularly good use on *The Generation Game*.)

These were the years in which Bruce built up an invaluable relationship with the British public. One of the reasons he has always been able to handle an audience so well is because he saw it up close and personal in the years before he became a star, and knows it so well. 'It's a family audience,' he said in an interview with *Radio Times* in 1972, 'the sort who might not bother to go to the theatre at home, but, being on holiday, they're different. The British on holiday love a bit of nonsense, a bit of a giggle, a bit of fun, and a good laugh.' As time went on, of course, that was exactly what the British audience wanted to watch on television, too – and Bruce was ideally placed to provide it. The slog and the grind finally were to pay off, as Bruce was to become popular and famous (and wealthy) beyond his dreams. But he wasn't there yet, and nor would he be for some time to come. Bruce still had quite an apprenticeship to serve.

The Windmill Years

IN THE LATE 1940s, Bruce's fortune began to change. Although nowhere near being a well known entertainer, Bruce had finally got to the stage of the Windmill Theatre in London's Soho, a venue that might surprise some of Bruce's family-oriented fans, given its decidedly racy past. Although tame in the extreme by today's standards, the Windmill Theatre sparked outrage in some quarters when it became Britain's first nude revue in the early 1930s, which is what it still was when Bruce came on board almost two decades later. Owned by Laura Henderson, who had managed to convince the Lord Chamberlain that women posing stark naked and totally still – they were never allowed to move – was high art, the Windmill also owed an enormous amount of its success to the theatrical impresario Vivian Van Damm. It was he who had to persuade the girls to pose naked.

Doris Barry – sister of the ballet dancer Dame Alicia Markova, and already a child star in her own right – was nineteen and touring in *Love Race*, when the director of that show asked her to audition for the Windmill in 1932. Tall and slim, she got the part and took it in her stride, despite starring in a show that crossed all the barriers of the day. She was not, however, one of the women who appeared nude.

'It was hard work, very hard work, but it was like a family,' she said in an interview with *The Stage*, conducted when she was ninety-two. 'You spent your life there. Van Damm was – and if I say dominant, I don't meant it in a nasty way – a very strong personality. He was very sexy, like the film star Walter Pidgeon.' The reason Van Damm came up with the idea for nude revues was that other venues had started staging shows five times a day, and business at the Windmill was looking bleak. So Van Damm decided they should stage five shows a day, too – with the unique selling point being the nude revues.

'It was a big thing,' said Doris, with commendable understatement. 'When we first heard, we all decided no way were we going to do that. We didn't want to be part of that. I was spokesgirl and I told him. But in his very prosaic, persuasive way, he said, "Now look, you have all been to the art gallery, the National Gallery, and seen these beautiful paintings. It is going to be like that". He said, "Why shouldn't the general public see these beautiful things?"'

The deal was done. Most of the show was made up of the theatre's famous fan dance and various other revues, but, before they came on, two women appeared naked and motionless on the stage. Male stagehands were banned from the wings. 'Nobody was bothered after five shows at the end of the first day,' said Doris but, especially with such a famous sister, she was aware that in some eyes, this was a very déclassé side of the profession.

'The Windmill Theatre was always rather looked down upon,' she said. 'I used to see people socially with my sister and they would say, "Good heavens, you work at the Windmill? I don't believe it", but then I would see them sitting there enjoying the show.'

Another of the dancers in the early days, also interviewed by *The Stage*, was Eileen Cruickshank; she was one of the women who appeared in the nude. After answering an advertisement in *The Stage*, she joined the theatre in 1936, where she found a sense of decorum ruled, which was essential if the Windmill was to present itself as good, middle-class entertainment, albeit with a rather racy edge.

'We just did this nude tableau for which we got extra

money, which was a great help in the war. We certainly didn't move,' she recalled. 'Occasionally, if you met someone, usually in the business, and you said you were at the Windmill, they would raise their eyebrows but not in a nasty way. [The costumes are] something that I always, always want to impress upon people. The Windmill was so beautifully done. The stage costumes were redesigned every six months, the material and the workshopping was so wonderful. I had been in musical comedies, which was a cut above revue, and the costumes were rubbish.' Eileen eventually left to work with the Bluebell Girls in Paris, before retraining as a nurse and marrying a doctor.

The Windmill Theatre was where Bruce wanted to go, but it took some time to get there. He finally established himself at the venue after the war, though he was first signed up for £10 a week while the war was still on. Shortly afterwards, he received his call-up papers and went to serve in the RAF. 'I really thought I was on top of the world when I did an audition at London's Windmill Theatre and was accepted,' he recalled in 1959. 'For two weeks I rehearsed hard, for one week I worked – and then the government began to take a great interest in my future and sent me my call-up papers.' Like his brother before him, Bruce joined the RAF.

By the time Bruce got to the Windmill on a more permanent basis, it had been operating as a nude revue establishment for over twenty years and Laura Henderson was long gone – she had died in 1944 and left it to Van Damm. Soho in the 1950s was not mainstream Britain: it was still a slightly shady place, but one that was in the heart of London's theatreland. It was a place to go and get noticed, and Bruce eventually did just that. 'I was back knocking at the Windmill door and getting another chance to learn that gags and gals can go together – if they're on at separate times,' he said.

The years Bruce spent at the Windmill provided some form of security in what was a notoriously unstable profession, as well as helping him to sharpen up his act. But it was gruelling stuff. 'After the war, I had a two-year spell at the Windmill Theatre learning my trade with six shows a day, six days a week,' he recalled in 1978. 'It was a good, steady job – you had your money every week.'

Bruce wasn't the only entertainer to learn his trade at the Windmill. Indeed, the line-up of those who started out at the Windmill reads like a veritable A–Z of British entertainment during those times: Peter Sellers, Harry Secombe, Michael Bentine, Kenneth More, Tony Hancock, Nicholas Parsons, Barry Cryer – all became household names. Bruce later remarked that there was no better training for a comedian than to face a different audience several times in the same day, especially when that audience had, primarily, come to see the girls.

One of the girls at the Windmill Theatre was to have an overwhelming influence on Bruce's life. A dancer called Penny Calvert, she was to become enmeshed with him both personally and professionally, as part of a singing and dancing double act – and as his first wife. While Bruce has clearly now found contentment with his third wife, it is often forgotten that he and Penny were married for twenty years, tying the knot in 1953. For her, at least, it was a *coup de foudre*. 'I saw this name, Bruce Forsyth, and suddenly there were green flashing lights in front of my eyes and I knew this was the man I was going to marry,' she later recalled.

Initially, it was work that drew them together. 'I took a hand in arranging the dances and music,' Bruce recalled to the *TV Times* 1959. 'One of the dancers I most enjoyed arranging for was Penny Calvert. We felt we were so well matched that we ought to strike out on our own. We didn't set the world on fire.' They were very young when they met, and perhaps Penny should have had an inkling of what their life was going to be like together for, right from the start, it was bound up with work. Not only did they meet through their professional lives, but their wedding and honeymoon were also linked to their work.

'The break came – an offer of a cabaret tour in India,' said Bruce. 'I gave the agent a ring to accept, and Penny a ring to get married. The wedding was in Edmonton and our honeymoon was a cruise through the Mediterranean. That's a nice way to start married life … even nicer when you aren't paying for it. India was idyllic, too. We used to turn up at the local European swimming club at 10am and stay there, diving in the water and drip drying in the sun, until eight at night when we'd get ready for the show.'

When the couple was still in India, one of those events happened that changes a person's life. Penny became ill. It was not the illness itself that changed everything, for Penny was to make a full recovery, but it did force the duo to reassess their act. Until then, it had been the two of them on stage, but with Penny struck down, Bruce had to go out and hold the show on his own. And he did, too. He didn't only sing and dance, there was spiel and patter. And it all came from him.

The audience loved it, and so Bruce, for the first time, began to think about trying out something else out.

This was to have profound implications for the marriage. Bruce was out on his own on stage – professionally, he didn't need Penny any more. Neither of them exactly realised what was happening – and it made it easier when Penny came to start having children.

In 1953, after returning to Britain, Bruce decided to strike out from The Windmill and change the emphasis of his act. He had until now been very much a cabaret performer, but decided to see if he could make a go of it as a comedian. It was a very brave move, and took some time before it paid off. 'It's been a feature of my career that I've always chosen my moments to get out and try something new, before I became stale,' he said.

He left steady work for something all together more uncertain. 'Back home in North London, I waited for my agent to fill my diary with variety dates, but for eight weeks there was nothing,' he told the *TV Times* in 1978. 'I was out of work, but I'd saved a few bob, so I could survive for a while. My mum and dad ran a family business in Edmonton, so I could always tap them for a couple of gallons of petrol. But it was a terrible feeling: you're raring to go, firing on all eight cylinders, and nobody wants you.'

It wasn't an ideal way to start family life, either. Bruce

had a caravan – which he used to tour up and down the country with Penny at his side – but no proper home of his own. It wasn't much fun. 'We used to tour in a caravan, because it was cheaper to live like that, in a semi-gypsy way,' he said. When they were in London, the couple stayed with Bruce's parents, who had become very attached to their daughter-in-law and who were only too happy to provide accommodation, but it was not ideal. If the couple were to build up a family together, then at some point they were going to need a house. It was out of the question for the moment, though: while Bruce was managing to put some money away, he had nowhere near enough for his own home.

Finally, at long last, Bruce got a booking. It was at the Brixton Empress in South London, and it was crucial Bruce made a good impression. 'I worked out a fifteen-minute act and rehearsed it,' he said. 'In those days, comics wrote their own material. It was vital that the show went well.'

It didn't. Bruce is unsparing in his recollection of the early days, and his is a salutary lesson to anyone who wants to make a career in show business. 'That week in Brixton was a total disaster,' he recalled. 'It was a big theatre, a glorified cinema, and very impersonal. But I'm not making excuses. I was so embarrassed about my reception I wouldn't even go to the canteen for a cup of tea with the other artists. I used to sneak in and out by the stage door.'

Bruce was talking about this in 1978, by which time he'd been one of the most popular entertainers in Britain for the best part of two decades, and it had clearly taken him that long to come to terms with what had happened. In 1959, shortly after his breakthrough, he also talked about his experience at Brixton, and while he certainly didn't claim it as a success, he didn't go into quite the searing detail he was later to recall. 'My "spot" – one of the most difficult in variety – was to do a comic turn immediately after the opening dance number,' he said. 'I was billed as a comedian, in other words. And most people could think of other words. They thought of them, as I remember, for the next two years. But gradually the name of Forsyth came to be recognised.'

At the time it seemed as if this might bring his career to a halt. 'My agent even had various impresarios in to see me, to advise me about where I was going wrong,' said Bruce. One of them said the trouble with Forsyth was that his voice was too high. He should try to lower it a couple of octaves and put on a pseudo-American accent, as they were all doing that at the Palladium. 'Well, I was so desperate I actually tried it,' explained Bruce. 'I bought a tape machine and practiced, trying to put on a deep brown voice with a Texan twang. It wasn't right for me.'

A lesser entertainer might have called it a day, but at that stage, aged twenty-five and newly married, Bruce had already been on the road for eleven years. He wasn't going to give up quite yet, and it was a measure of his determination that he didn't, because it was going to take another five years before he finally got his big break. It is as well we cannot see into the future: he had years of slog yet to come.

Ernie and Doreen Wise – the Ernie of Morecombe and Wise – knew Bruce back in those days, when they were all struggling. 'He was always restless,' Ernie re-called in 1992. 'Very anxious to get on and make it. But he was kind.'

In later years, he was asked if he had an ego. 'If you haven't got an ego, you shouldn't be in show business,' he said. 'You've got to think you've got something the public wants, to give you the courage to go out there. That doesn't mean you're like that all the time, that when you come off stage you don't criticise yourself. You can't let the ego become egotistical and you can't begin to think that everything you do is magic. When you stop being nervous, you stop being a true performer. But the trick is not to let anyone know how you really feel. I take the other Bruce out of the box and push him on. Go on, get out there. And he's got it all; he has a smile on his face. He'll pick on people. He'll do his opening song. But underneath, there's that little person saying: "Will you like me tonight?"'

Ever the professional, as soon as the Brixton slot was over, Bruce was back on the road again. 'I finished at Brixton on Saturday night, got out in one piece, and on the Sunday motored up to my next date, in Leeds,' he continued. 'My Austin 10 was stacked with props for my act. The show at the City Varieties was to be called *This'll Make You Wink*, with a mixed variety bill of jugglers, acrobats, comics – and nudes. Topping the bill was the comic Dave King who was, of course, to make it very big in the next few years.'

Not as big as Bruce, of course, but the man himself was aware that it was crucial he got his act right. Otherwise, he might not get another chance. 'I stayed in a little boarding house in Cobden Place,' he continued. 'Nice digs they were, too, unlike some, where the landlady would bring you a hard pork pie and fourteen peas and call it supper. Full board for seven nights cost £1.10s and the theatre was paying me £20 for twelve performances. It was Christmas week and Leeds was decked out with decorations, but it could have been the middle of June for all I knew. After that terrible week at Brixton, I could only think of one thing: to get my act right. If I had another week like the last one, I don't know what I'd have done. I might have cut my losses and gone back to the safety of revue.'

Even for such an experienced performer as he then was, Bruce was in a state. He was due to go on stage on 21 December 1953, and it was this night that he really felt would make or break him for good. He couldn't go on living with his parents forever, nor could he go on earning next to nothing. Bruce continued to reflect on the terror he was feeling before he finally went out on to the stage.

'Anybody who has made a speech at a wedding knows how the shivers creep down your spine when you get up on your own,' he reminisced. 'Going on stage in a chorus, or as part of a double act, you don't feel that same sort of panic. Nothing quite matches the pressure on the solo comic. Call it guts, courage, or a super-big ego; you need a special quality to get out there on your own. A singer can always finish his song, and even if he's rotten, the audience will wait till the end before they give him a derisory patter of applause. But the comedian gets his reaction – a laugh, a chuckle, or a stony, lonely silence – after every line. He needs a reaction flowing back from the audience to spark off his next line. That's why I have always said comedy is the hardest profession of all. No one suffers quite like the bad comic.' If he failed this time round, then this aspect of his life was going to be over for good.

He didn't. Much in the manner of a good fictional drama, Bruce, with absolutely everything to play for, finally pulled it off, developing the style that was to become his trademark. 'Apart from a string of quick-fire gags, my act that night in Leeds was visual,' he recalled. 'I used to do impressions of different people – such as the reactions of a tramp or a toff on finding a half crown. Anyway, my most vivid memory of that night was one thing – applause. My act was no different from the one I'd done at Brixton, but perhaps I'd shown more confidence, perhaps I'd transmitted a more relaxed mood to the audience. But I got the same warm response from the second house, and for the rest of the week.'

It was a night that transformed Bruce's fortunes, his career, and his life. For the first time, he'd had reassurance that he could make it on his own on the stage, could carry an audience, and could keep the gags coming, one after another. It was what he needed to know and, with hindsight, it is possible to see that it was this experience that worked so incredibly well when he came to do *Sunday Night at the London Palladium*. 'It was a marvellous Christmas present,' said Bruce. 'I felt so encouraged. I knew that after that week at the *City Varieties* I could make my way as a comic. As I drove back from Leeds, I was bubbling with a new confidence, ready for my next date at the Metropolitan on Edgware Road in London. While I was there, I was spotted by the BBC and offered my first television date, on a show called *Music Hall*.'

The work he did then was to prove invaluable. 'You knew how to work to a family audience,' he said in an interview just before his eightieth birthday. 'Comics today don't get the chance; they have to work in comedy clubs, which are very abrasive. But when you worked in variety, you couldn't even say "bloody" or the Lord Chamberlain would be round. Morecambe and Wise, Frankie Howerd, Tommy Cooper: they all had a certain warmth of performance that's maybe lacking today.'

Ronnie Corbett, whose breakthrough also took some time, first met Bruce when they were appearing in Danny la Rue's nightclub in Hanover Square. He is convinced that the long apprenticeship was helpful. 'These days, you get a series when you're twenty-three,' he said, pointing out that a long background in variety was perfect training for his generation. 'It made us look comfortable on our feet,' he said.

He was probably right; for all his playing around with the audience, Bruce has always had a certain warmth. It was this work that finally set him on the path to success. It led to a season in Babbacombe, Devon, after which Bruce got a slot on the show that temporarily replaced *Palladium*: *Sunday Night at the Prince of Wales*. He was about to burst on to the scene.

At this stage there were no problems between Bruce and Penny. The marriage, which technically lasted for twenty years, produced the first three of Bruce's six children – Debbie, Julie, and Laura – and was happy enough to start off with. Debbie was born on 24 June 1955, while Julie arrived on 4 April 1958, the year of Bruce's big break. It was also a time of some personal sadness – Bruce's mother Florence died in 1957 at the age of sixty-three, not living to witness the huge star her son would become. Bruce's father, however, did see his boy make his breakthrough and in fact married again – to Florence's sister Dolly – an arrangement that clearly did not upset the rest of the family, who were relieved that John had solace and company in his old age.

Even with the personal happiness his children brought him and the fact that his career was finally moving up a gear, it was not an easy life, especially in the breaks between jobs. 'Those were terrible times,' Bruce said years later. 'The frustration: that was the worst thing of all. I once gave myself five years. I seemed to be going nowhere. I used to come off stage and one of my mates would be in the wings and he'd ask, "Any good?" meaning the audience, and I'd shake my head and say, "No". You do despair, you do get down in spirit. I said to myself, "If things don't change in five years, I'm packing it in". But you soon snap out of it. Or rather, I did, I'm happy to say.'

But, post Leeds, he was finally on his way. There were a number of stages in Bruce's early career that played a significant part in his life, namely the Windmill Theatre, Leeds, and now the place that was to play an enormously important role in his progress to the top. It was Babbacombe, near Torquay in Devon, which in the summer would be filled with holidaymakers, all keen for exactly the sort of family entertainment that Bruce personified. Geographically, he was in the right place, as it was where Bruce was spotted for *Sunday Night at the London Palladium*. It was also where he was to learn more about his trade and to cement his ability to handle an audience, including getting members of the public to come and perform on stage. His bosses back then realised his worth: Bruce was awarded Babbacombe's 'Bucket and Spade Oscar' in 1956 and 1957 for his antics at the Babbacombe Concert Hall.

He earned it, too. 'You'd have to learn about twenty-four sketches during each season, apart from all the jokes and quickies,' he recalled. 'I was principal comic. There would also be a leading lady, the pianist, the drummer, and three dancing girls, and that would be about all. So when I say experience, I really mean experience. After three years there, I had an absolute wealth of material. They would be old sketches that had been going around for years, but I've always had quite a creative mind for ad libs in sketches, and finding a better tag for them.'

It was here that Bruce, for the first time, experienced 'give away' shows. 'That was my first taste of audience participation,' he said. 'And I found I really did like that, not knowing what would happen next. I've realised since, not only with *Palladium* and "Beat the Clock", but also *The Generation Game*, that this is another field of entertainment for me to work in. At the time, I just treated it as a giggle, a bit of mucking about. But it has been very important since.'

Bruce's professional life was to be transformed when he attracted the attention of talent scouts for Val Parnell. He was, after sixteen years in the business, about to become an overnight success. It was, of course, when he was picked to host *Sunday Night at the London Palladium*, and in the very best traditions of show business, Bruce was to achieve what is every entertainer's great dream. He was to walk on to the stage a complete unknown and leave it a star.

I'm In Charge!

BRUCE FORSYTH WAS a star. The year was 1958 and, overnight, he had become the biggest name on television. As host of *Sunday Night at the London Palladium*, Bruce had finally achieved all the fame and fortune that he wanted – and more. And *Sunday Night at the London Palladium* was the perfect vehicle for him: a variety show that combined audience participation with games such as 'Beat the Clock', and a guest list that featured some of the most famous performers of the day. The show had been running for some time before Bruce joined it, but it could have been put together with him in mind.

'It took me sixteen years,' he said. 'I didn't just do a hit record, or appear on a show where everyone knows you even if you're not a performer [i.e. reality television]. That's why everyone today wants to be a presenter. Sixteen years before you hit it big is a long time.' Before fame, he admitted, he was always very eager to see the newspapers. 'As a nobody, you just wanted to see if you were mentioned, if someone had said you were good or that you'd tried your best.'

Bruce remembered it fondly in the run-up to his eightieth birthday. 'I took over from the late Tommy Trinder, and I still remember the first one that I did,' he said. 'There was Jewell and Warris, the most successful double act of their day; the singers Anne Shelton and David Whitfield; and a young comic called Peter Sellers. They were all so nice to me, and their encouragement was an enormous help. I started off doing it for £85 a week, but because I made a success of it, my pay went up, not long after, to £1000 a week, which was unheard of in TV terms those day.' He was petrified on the first night, though. 'I had to drive round the block three times before I went on,' he recalled. 'So much depended on it – my future career and my family.'

Michael Grade, controller of both LWT and BBC1, and chief executive of Channel 4, the BBC and ITV, is a huge admirer of Bruce, originally encountering him (Bruce) when he was a child. 'He took the nation by storm,' he said. 'He was magical. He'd do "Beat the Clock", then Sammy Davis Jr. or Nat King Cole would come out and he'd hold his own with them. I've never seen anyone like him before or since. He's been a star longer than anyone.'

This was not, actually, Bruce's first acquaintance with the show. In 1957, he had had a spot on the show, when Tommy Trinder had been in charge. Bruce's own leap to stardom all came about because Val Parnell, who was in charge of the Palladium, was looking for a new host for the *Sunday Night* show. 'I was doing summer season at Babbacombe and some friends of mine – Francois and Zandra, who did a novelty dancing act – persuaded Billy Marsh, an agent who worked for Bernard Delfont, to come and see me,' Bruce recalled. It worked: Billy Marsh persuaded Parnell that here was a new and rare talent. Bruce was offered a six-week contract – and the rest, as they say, is history. Bruce was to host the show for two years, followed by a year's break, followed by another year back on the show.

One of the reasons Bruce had been thought of for the Palladium was because of one of the turns he'd done at the Prince of Wales. Bruce had the last slot, and was due to go on for five minutes. However, just before he went on stage, the producers asked if he could stay on a little longer than usual as the show was not quite on schedule. 'I did as I was told and, as I was getting to the end of my act, I got frantic "hurry up" signals,' Bruce recalled to the *TV Times* in 1959. 'Later I learned why. I had been on for nine-and-a-half minutes – and the top star usually gets only eight or nine minutes. It certainly got me talked about and was one of the things that led to my being given the *Palladium* job. When discussions were held about a new compere for the *Palladium* show, Bernard Delfont recalled my Prince of Wales effort.'

Bruce's ability to deal with a crisis was not the only reason his name came to mind. There was another element of *Sunday Night...* that was particularly difficult to do, and needed someone who could improvise, put people at their ease, and deal with any problems that might arise, live on air. It was the segment 'Beat the Clock'. 'More was needed than a good compere – they wanted someone capable of tackling the complicated "Beat the Clock",' Bruce recalled. 'This is unscripted and calls for the ability to deal with people who have never been on stage before. Billy Marsh, one of the Delfont organisation, recalled seeing one of my Babbacombe shows, where I had my own quiz and spent more time chatting to people than getting on with the games. They decided to give me a trial.'

Those games were a fantastic preparation for the real thing. During the week, it was a normal variety show, but on Sundays, because of the Observance laws, the show became something called a 'plain clothes concert'. To help fill in the time, Bruce would get on with those games, giving out tiny items as prizes. 'We gave away tea caddies, things like that, worth about 7s 6d. I used to say to the winners, "If you were on telly this would be a washing machine", but I never dreamed I'd be doing it myself on TV one day.' And, of course, he had to make quite a leap from playing a tiny audience to playing a vast one. 'I had to learn to cut the theatre down to my size, you see,' he said. 'It was quite a jump from the eight-hundred-seat theatre in Eastbourne to over two thousand in the Palladium. And for television, you've got to bring it down to the size of someone's front room.'

The trial run turned out to be a spectacular success, though Bruce very nearly brought matters to an end before they'd properly begun. He has been very astute in his career decisions throughout much of his life, but despite his massive popularity, he very nearly walked out on the show before he had become properly established. It was a decision he had to be talked out of, and Val Parnell was the man to save Bruce from himself. After the initial four weeks, Bruce was called in to discuss his contract – and said he wanted to walk.

'When Val Parnell told me he liked the way I was do-ing the show and wanted to extend the booking, I decided to put my cards on the table,' Bruce recalled in 1959. 'I stuck out my chin – which is hard to do as it's usually stick-ing out on its own – and said, "I want to quit". The idea of staying on worried me. I'd heard that too much television was bad for an artist, and I didn't want people getting tired of me. Maybe that sounds a bit strange coming from someone just reaching up to the heights of stardom. I just felt that way. Val Parnell, however, wouldn't hear of it. He said nice things about new faces and public interest and staying on to the end of June. I left his office with my head in a whirl. When he'd been complimenting me on my handling of the show, his voice seemed to take on a bell-like quality. But when I figured that June was thirty shows away, I forgot about the bell and just reckoned I must have been cracked to accept.' As it happens, he wasn't. It was the making of his career.

He first realised he was famous in a rather bizarre way. 'I'd been listed in two polls in the red-top newspapers,' Bruce recalled. 'One was for the people on TV that you most loved, and the other was for the people you most hated. It was hilarious. I rang my old mate, the comic and writer Barry Cryer and I said, "Barry, I've cracked it!"'

In an interview with *The Evening News*, conducted by Kendall McDonald back in 1958, Bruce seemed quite overwhelmed by it all. This was one of his first major interviews, and although he has had many years since then to get used to the success that so suddenly swept him off his feet, this interview took place when it was all still fresh. His first season at *Sunday Night...* had just ended and he was now appearing in the Palladium's pantomime as Presto the Jester.

'If 1959 is anything like the last few months of 1958, then I can hardly wait for 1959,' he said. 'My income has been gradually rising during my work in summer seasons and the like, but now it is trebled. A year ago, we bought a new house at St Albans. But now I am so rarely out of London that we are looking for a house in town. You know all this has rather swept me off my feet. It's marvellous. I'd lived in London all my life. Before this, I could walk about like any ordinary chap, go into shops and be unnoticed. Now, everybody talks to me. Taxi drivers, the lot. I couldn't believe it at first.'

It was a case of dreams coming true, and although Bruce was not always to adopt such a conciliatory note with the press, at this stage he simply seemed overawed by his great good luck. 'This is giving me a chance to do something that I always wanted to do,' he continued. 'Musical comedy. People say, "You're like Tommy Trinder or Jack Hulbert". It's the chin, you know. Ever since I was small, I idolised Jack Hulbert. I used to imitate him. That's the sort of line I'd like to go along. Musical comedy. I've been dancing like this since I was eleven. I'd like to do everything. Musical comedy, light comedy, straight variety.' As for his material: 'I had plenty of chance to stockpile in the summer season. I write my own material. That gag about the drip-dry shirt, for example. You wouldn't think people would take the trouble. Look at this.' And he motioned to a tiny, replica drip-dry shirt.

The viewers loved him. He had a way of communicating directly with them, and the audience, so while he was, on the one hand, a talented stage performer, he was also one of them. And he appeared so normal: married with two children – Debbie was three when he shot to fame, and Julia was just a few months old – and a dog called Rusty. He was a natural and a pro.

The whole family revelled in his success at that stage, with Bruce poring over the critics with an almost childlike glee. '"The cheeky boy on the bacon counter," he called me,' he said of one. 'I loved that! It's a family joke, now. If Penny catches me trying on something, teasing her, she says, "There's that cheeky boy on the bacon counter again". Another critic called me television's end-of-the-pier comic. I like that, too. The end-of-the-pier comic has to work hard on his audience, make them feel they're all having fun together, having a good time! I've always tried to do the same with the *Palladium* audience – I mean all the viewers at home – make them feel they're really there.'

His handling of contestants was by turns gentle and aggressive, but he never wounded and never went over the top. Bruce's career has been characterised by catchphrases, and the first of these now appeared: 'I'm in charge!' Audiences loved it and so did he – after such a long slog, gaining the popularity he'd always longed for was thrilling. He was on a roll.

The catchphrase actually came about by chance, and it provided Bruce with an invaluable insight into what did and didn't work on television. 'One of the things that has most impressed me about television is the way you let something slip casually and find it isn't a remark you've dropped so much as a brick,' he said in 1959. 'Or a catchphrase that sweeps the country. I never set out to originate anything with this line, but it looks as though I'm saddled with, "I'm in charge!" and gags about drip-dry shirts for life.'

'The story of IIC goes back to a "Beat the Clock" game in November 1958. I explained to a young couple how to play a game involving plate throwing. They got in a terrible state – there were plates flying all over the place. If the whole thing had taken place years earlier, I doubt if flying saucers would ever have caught on. Anyway, I stopped the clock and said, "Look, throw them one at a time, alternately, and you'll be all right." I turned around to see how many seconds they had left and would you believe it, in a twink they were off again slinging plates one at a time – one handful at a time! So I shouted, "Hold on, I'm in charge!"'

'I never have understood why it got such a big laugh. But there it was – a catchphrase was born. Only I didn't realise it. The following week I had forgotten all about it. But others hadn't. The show had hardly finished before I was being asked, "What's up, Bruce? Aren't you in charge any more?" That's when I realised it might be a good gimmick.'

Indeed, the phrase became something of a national craze for years, and remains, to this day, one with which Bruce is closely associated. People used it, everywhere, both in connection with Bruce and also on their own. 'I heard about a hole in a road in Birmingham, around which workmen had painted, "I'm in charge!"' Bruce recalled. 'Then there was the factory, where the workmen pinned a card on the back of their foreman's overalls, announcing, "He's in charge". In an exclusive Manchester restaurant I found the immaculately dressed manager wearing an apron on which he had written my catchphrase. Autograph hunters demand I sign their books, "Bruce Forsyth, IIC".'

The IIC catchphrase, like the gags about drip-dry shirts, started to follow him everywhere, including in his own show. Bruce was now so popular that he could go out on the road, under his name alone, and be guaranteed a full house. The audience knew what they wanted, and got it, too. 'It grew so much it became the title of my touring stage show,' said Bruce. 'One theatre advertised it simply as, "Bruce Forsyth is in charge".'

The drip-dry routine is not so well remembered now, but back then people loved it. 'What about that drip-dry shirt gag?' asked Bruce. 'It started off to fill in twenty seconds. I said, "Aren't these drip-dry shirts just marvellous? No ironing. Just wash them and put them on. Do you know, this one is nearly dry now. Mind you – my shoes are full of water". That started it – a cascade of comebacks from the customers. 'It's your fault if your shoes are full of water – you should wear drainpipe trousers ... Why don't you wear pumps? ... Wear a leek in your button-hole ... You shouldn't do so much tap dancing". I thought the gags would never stop.'

To say Bruce loved his new life would be an under-statement: it was everything he'd ever dreamed of and more. As time went on, audiences loved him more, not less. That drip-dry gag is a perfect example of why Bruce did so well in his new role: he took an every day, cur-rent concern with which his audience would have been familiar, made a silly joke about it, and then encouraged audience participation on the back of it. The only wonder was that it had taken him so long to reach the top.

Of course, the contestants on 'Beat the Clock' were also a huge part of the show's success. 'Beattie,' recalled Bruce in 1972. 'She died only recently. She came on to "Beat the Clock" and she just never stopped talking. Well, that was on the *Sunday Night* TV show. I was ap-pearing in the Palladium panto at the time during the week, and when I made a joke – for the boys in the band, really – about Beattie, the whole Monday matinee audi-ence just roared with laughter. That was when I realised the power of television, discovering that someone could become known to millions overnight, as Beattie did, because she couldn't stop talking. That was quite a shock to me.'

Looking back on it, Bruce was very aware of what a huge change this represented in his life. 'It was my biggest break,' he said more recently. 'It was live and the biggest job on TV and, within months, I was one of the best-known faces on television. People would leave pubs at 7.30pm to go home and see it. I signed on for forty weeks and did the Palladium pantomime at the same time. Life is that much easier for performers nowadays, with shows being filmed or taped. In the late Fifties, it was live, which is much more demanding on performers. But if you got into a problem, you just found a way out of it. I think it's a bit too easy now.'

Bruce was now very famous indeed, but he did not let it go to his head. George Cooper, the long-serving stage doorkeeper at the Palladium, remembered those days in an interview in 1972. 'Bruce is not one of those troublesome stars; he doesn't ask for special favours,' he said. 'I think the secret of his success is his charm, the way he can put people at their ease. He has this wonderful cheery face that he presents to the world.'

'I am a bit good at many things,' Bruce said. 'I love making people laugh. My comedy inspiration was Max

Miller. When I was a kid, he was probably the most ris-
qué comedian of the time. But his was not like the cru-
dity you get today. There was always a double meaning
to what Max said. I loved his style, delivery, connection
with the audiences.'

Bruce was also a great admirer of the dancers of the
day. 'Fred Astaire was the master,' he said. 'He had an
edge on them because he was so elegant, he just had to
walk a few steps and it was like watching someone dance.
I had the great pleasure of working with Nat King Cole,
best known as a singer, but he was also a brilliant pianist.
He was a wonderful person. The best TV show I ever did
was with Sammy Davis Jr. I played for him when he sang,
he played for me when I sang, and when people come to
visit now and I show them the tape, it still stands up as a
good show.'

In later years, he actually looked back on that show
with some wistfulness, thinking of a different kind of career from the one he ended up having. 'I always feel I
would like to have done more entertainment shows like
the one I did with Sammy Davis Jr.,' he said. 'I just love
doing a show where there's music, where I danced and
had fun with someone, and worked with a big star. I will
always feel I didn't do enough of those sort of shows.'

His other regret from that time is that he never worked with Frank Sinatra. 'Sinatra never worked the Palladium, and I only met him once, very briefly, when he was appearing at the Festival Hall and my daughter Julie was in a group called Guys and Dolls, who were on the bill with him,' Bruce said. 'Julie introduced us in the corridor before the show. I'm sure he had his eye on her, actually. Very attractive girl, my daughter.'

However, *Sunday Night at the London Palladium* was the making of him and now, at last, the full range of experience he'd built up over the years was being put to work. Quite simply, Bruce could do anything. He could sing, dance, bully and cajole the audience, switch into game show mode, and then come on with all the panache of a Broadway trouper. Nothing phased him, and he just about never put a foot wrong.

Possibly the most famous episode during his tenure on the show came when the actors' union Equity called a strike for a week, from which Bruce and the comedian Norman Wisdom were exempt. No one else was able to appear. To the delight of the audience, between them, improvising away, they managed to last out the entire show. It was a night that went down in show business history.

As the audience grew to dote on this tall, angular tap dancer with the common touch, they showed their appreciation vividly, too, starting with that drip-dry gag. 'The gifts!' Bruce revealed in 1959. 'In came shoals of plastic buckets, clotheslines, packets of detergent, bundles of pegs. Children sent paper cut-out shirts. There was a never-ending supply of tiny, drip-dry shirts with my initials. My dressing room was packed with so many gifts that Father Christmas asked me for my union card!'

'I once received a haggis all dressed up in a paper kilt,' said Bruce. 'When I showed it on the show, just like the nervous amateur it went all to pieces. Literally! Waiting for me at the Palladium the next week was a tartan wheelbarrow with the message, "This is a haggis carrier". Now this surprised me, for I always thought a haggis carrier was a Scotsman with a full stomach. Remember the time I casually mentioned that my car was not running so well? I was inundated by a fleet of toy cars of all shapes, materials, and sizes. Somebody sent a handle. Another, a toy rope. And a do-it-yourself tuning kit. To cap the lot came a full-scale car, which we showed on the programme in November and passed on to an old folks' welfare organisation.' Meanwhile, he was getting rich, earning a then absolutely colossal £1,000 per show, and moving with his family to a large home in north London. As he himself admitted, not so long ago he wasn't able to earn that in a whole year.

Bruce's whole life was changing now, not just in terms of his fame, but his standard of living, too. His income meant that the years of grafting were over, and he could finally indulge himself in a way he hadn't been able to in the past. 'The first thing I bought was a new car,' he recalled. 'I'd always wanted an estate car, one big enough to carry all my stuff as I was travelling around the country.' In addition, he relished 'being able to go to places I wanted to go to, and being able to pay for a nice meal in a nice restaurant, without worrying about the bill.' Not that the bill was always such an issue. He'd go in, he said, 'dying to pay the bill, but head waiters would say, "Have this with our compliments". If I'd gone in there a few years earlier as a starving actor begging for a roll and butter, I'm sure they would have chucked me out.'

Bruce was also getting used to being recognised everywhere he went. In these days of instant celebrity, where everyone wants to be famous without having much of an idea what they want to be famous for, it's sometimes easy to forget that not so long ago, celebrity was a by-product of achievement, not an end in itself. Though it still had its drawbacks. 'At first, it was marvellous,' said Bruce in an interview in the 1970s. 'Then sometimes it was a bit of a nuisance. But you had to learn to accept it and enjoy it and not let yourself be hung-up about it. I just enjoy it, now.'

He had, wisely, prepared himself for all this by never allowing himself to become morose in the many years on the road before he finally made it. 'I never got bitter, you know,' he said. 'I would have hated that. You used to see them a lot, the bitter comics. You'd arrive at a theatre all eager and ready to go and they'd look down their noses at you. A disdainful look it was – strangely creepy, almost. It said, "Don't fool yourself, kid, in another ten years you'll end up just like me." Thank God I didn't.'

Bruce was careful to eschew other temptations, too. From an early stage, he developed rigid self-control, something that no doubt contributes to him still being able to go on stage in his eighties. While other entertainers have ruined themselves by allowing a fondness for alcohol to become a habit, Bruce was always very careful. 'I used to keep a glass filled up with wine in the wings,' he once related. 'But one night when I was doing a lot of dashing on and off stage, I totted it up and discovered I had drunk about three-quarters of a bottle. So I gave it up. I figure that if you're the only sober person in the theatre, you've got a head start.'

'I had seen it all you see, in the sixteen years before it happened to me. I'd seen the gambling, the drinking, the wasted lives. If I hadn't, how would I, how could I, have coped? It would have been like winning the pools. But I had seen the unhappiness it could bring. It wasn't going to happen to me. I didn't want to squander my good fortune. I wanted my roots to go six feet deep. Sixteen years is a long time to wait.'

Indeed, he would treat his performances as a fighter did in the ring. 'I suppose it is like a fight, taking on an audience,' he said. 'You've got to prepare yourself for it. For instance, I will always have an early dinner. I never take any food or alcohol for four hours before I go on because it slows me down. People you meet think you're being rude, turning down their offers of drinks and dinner, but there it is, it can't be helped.' It was clear: nothing was going to get in the way of the job.

His routine was to become a fixed one: he would gargle with Cockburns port, as it was good for the throat. When he did drink, it was in moderation; he didn't smoke; he took vitamins and pollen tablets, and would put lemon and honey in his tea to help his throat. And he took his lucky mascot everywhere: a little sailor doll given to him by three chorus girls many years previously at the Windmill Theatre. Bruce was also constantly monitoring himself. Now that he was at the top, he fully intended to stay there. 'Every second that I'm on I'm watching myself and them,' he said, 'marking myself, giving myself a pat on the back or a kick in the pants.'

But with such instant and huge success, something had to give, and it did. Bruce later acknowledged that having finally got what he always wanted, professionally, he clung on with both hands – and his marriage suffered as a result. Work was everything to him, and when he wasn't on television, he was appearing elsewhere. It was a classic case of a performer from humble roots being terrified that he would be banished back to them. His relationship with Penny was suffering as a result.

'That kind of overnight success is difficult to handle,' he said. 'It's like winning the lottery – you've absolutely no idea how it is going to affect you. Before *Palladium* happened I had a period of fourteen weeks out of work with nothing coming in from anywhere. When you've lived like that for years, you can't help thinking, "Is all this going to finish?" You have to grab it with both hands. Your personal life has to take a back seat. It's bound to affect your marriage.' It did. Penny later complained that she covered herself in perfume, lit candles, and put on a negligee in a bid to relight her husband's interest. 'Bruce came back from the Palladium and said: "It was a terrible audience tonight. I'm going to bed". He didn't even notice,' she later recalled. But he was to notice other women – to devastating effect.

Ladies' Man

BRUCE MIGHT NOT have been paying as much attention to Penny as he once did, but he certainly noticed what was happening to his career. Audiences everywhere adored him, and after a few hugely successful years on *Sunday Night...*, clocking up a record twenty-four-and-a-half million viewers for one show, along with his own touring shows, he went on to be awarded a television show all of his own. Broadcast on Saturday nights, it was called *Bruce's Show*, and the fact that he didn't even need his surname in the title was a reflection of just how well known he'd become.

'The Bruce Forsyth of the spectacular *Palladium* shows has gone,' he said in an interview with the *TV Times* in 1962. 'The keynote to this series will be intimacy, projecting Bruce Forsyth in a more chatty, personal setting, getting together with celebrities. I am a little worried whether the audience will go along with me. But, if I continued to perform as before, they soon would have tired of seeing the old Bruce in the old pattern.' This was, mark you, just four years after his initial success, and yet already there was an 'old Bruce'. It had been less than half a decade since he had got to the top, and yet by now it was impossible for him to imagine the world of light entertainment behind him.

This was to be an absolutely manic time in Bruce's life. As he himself admitted many, many times in later years, he was a difficult man to live with back then, utterly dedicated to his career. In his third and most successful marriage, he put his wife first; Penny, however, did not have a similar experience. As Bruce admitted several decades later, he was not a faithful husband. Perhaps it was the delight in finally finding himself in the limelight after so many years of struggle; perhaps it was simply that his marriage wasn't strong enough to resist the many temptations on offer to a famous entertainer. In any case, this was the time when his first marriage really began to fall apart.

'The only thing in life I take seriously is being funny,' he announced. 'Comedy is the one vital issue. And now that I have started my own weekly series on TV, I must sit back and try to analyse my particular approach and where I am going with it. I really cannot define myself as a comedian because that is not how I think of myself. I am an entertainer. I don't set out to make people laugh. I try to keep them happy and often keep them amused in the process, but that is a different thing.'

'I can sing, dance, chatter patter, crack gags, spin stories, but, basically, I am not a singer, a dancer, or a funster,' he continued. 'I merely use these accomplishments as a background around which I weave a unified act. I try to fashion something that is uniquely me – and hence different from any other performer – out of a great many of these ingredients. In the same way, when I was compere of *Sunday Night at the London Palladium*, I did not see myself as a comic compere. I tried to be different. I did not tell a single story. I alternated a string of patter and incidents about myself with musical numbers. I even worked with several artists appearing in the show. Some people thought that was a cheek. The stars were top billers; I was compere. Yet to me it was a form of entertainment – and a successful one.'

That was actually a perfectly accurate analysis of Bruce's act and remains an accurate description of his performances to this day. Above all, he was very aware of the importance of audience interaction, another indicator of why he has managed to stay at the top for so long.

'I need the audience to be a part of everything I do,' he said. 'The approval of those who know me is not enough. I must have the respect of all those strangers to whom I am playing. I think the audience participation in the fullest sense is very good for the comedian. That's why, although this new show is standard – musical numbers, sketches, and guest stars – I am interviewing also a lot of ordinary people, talking to them about their work and lives. After each show, we talk to the audience about themselves and what they have seen, and we tape their ideas. Perhaps we shall incorporate some of this into future shows.'

Although he appeared to be totally spontaneous, in the background, Bruce had done his homework. Nothing was left to chance. It was a pattern he was to stick to for the rest of his life. Of course, on top of that, he also had a quite exceptional ability to think on his feet, but Bruce never winged it, never failed to put in the work behind the scenes. It was a type of professionalism that was to stand him in extremely good stead.

While his marriage was soon to encounter serious dif-ficulties, there was very good news on the home front when, on 19 November 1962, Penny gave birth to the couple's third child, Laura. Bruce was thrilled. To the outside world at least, it looked as if he had achieved domestic, as well as professional, contentment. The family continued to lead an increasingly prosperous life: although Penny was to accuse Bruce of meanness in later years, they were very comfortably off. But there were a few elements that would eventually pull them apart permanently: Bruce's continuing obsession with his career; Penny's very hot, Irish temper; and Bruce's roving eye.

Now that Bruce was rich and famous, he increasingly was becoming a magnet to women. He had never had the slightest difficulty in attracting female company, but it's a well-known belief that women are drawn to powerful men, and so the more successful Bruce became, the more women were attracted to him. And temptation was everywhere. When he wasn't working in London, he was constantly out on the road, while Penny stayed at home and looked after the children. No longer could she accompany him in their caravan across the country – her motherly duties came first.

Above all, Bruce was concerned about his career – which, more than any woman, was truly his first love at that time. As preparations continued for the new show, Bruce continued to revel in his popularity and status as one of the country's most loved entertainers. There was increasing curiosity about this man who had leapt from nowhere to become one of the best-known faces in Britain: what was the secret to it all? 'I suppose it must be my ability to get on with people and my sense of humour,' mused Bruce in 1962.

He also continued to keep a keen eye on who else was out there and how they compared – this was also to stand him in spectacularly good stead in the early Noughties when his acquaintance with Paul Merton led to yet another renaissance in his career. It was a habit that dated right back to the start of his professional life.

'I admire the pace-men most,' he said, and it must be said, he was one of those himself. 'Those with fast minds and quick speech, like that zany idiot, Harry Secombe. He doesn't work the way I do, straight to an audience. He either sings seriously or works off his comedy with a group of people, bouncing his lines from one to the other. He wears me out even more that I wear out myself. Comedy that is unexpected appeals to me, like Bilko. And I have grown up loving the old gagsters like Bob Hope. But while I can laugh at them, I cannot model my style on theirs, which is something my scriptwriters have to learn.'

With that last remark, it was becoming clear that Bruce was not only certain about his own specific style, but was also a lot more confident about demanding what he wanted. The Bruce of a previous years would have leapt at whatever material he was being offered, but the Bruce of 1962 was a different kettle of fish. While retaining the man of the people aura that made him so popular with audiences, he was becoming an increasing perfectionist behind the scenes, and was very aware of his growing status and what he expected from the people he worked with. Not that he'd turned into a difficult man.

'The most important relationship in one's working life is with the scriptwriters,' he said. 'Sid Green and Derek Hills, who are scripting my new show, have worked with me for a long time. They are right for me, and so, inevitably, they come up with the right situations. The partnership is a 50/50 one. They think up some of the situations, I think up others, and we hammer them out fully at rehearsals. Occasionally, when everything is planned perfectly and I am on stage, I go mad and leave the script entirely. It turns the writers into nervous wrecks.'

The writers weren't the only ones. Home life was increasingly unhappy: Penny's volatile Irish temperament constantly made itself felt, as did Bruce's ongoing obsession with his career. He was also willing to admit that there was a darker side to him. 'The idea of that happy bloke we all feel at home with is true, I suppose,' he said. 'But it is a high-powered projection of my better qualities. I am, by nature, not always happy. I suffer intense bouts of depression. I am incredibly restless. The catch phrase, "I'm in charge", though it arose purely by accident, actually reflects another side of my personality – the irritable, domineering side that viewers don't often see. The thing that irritates me above all is incompetence. And it is the thing I try to guard against most of all. If I can be nothing else, I can, at least, be efficient.'

But trouble was beginning to stir in the background. While Bruce might have been increasingly unreceptive to Penny, he was by no means unaware of the charms of the other women he encountered, the women who were now beginning to throw themselves at him. Although he will not boast about conquests, he was a ladies' man, and, until his third marriage, never really calmed down. 'The thing is, I do like women's company more than men's,' he said in one interview, although in fairness he was talking about a general attitude rather than extra marital flings. 'There's nothing more boring than being at a dinner party where all the blokes want to do is tell jokes. Women talk about anything and everything.'

Penny had been ambitious, too, and it must have been

extremely difficult for her to watch her marriage fall apart as her husband went on to achieve ever more. Michael Grade summed it up. 'I think he was very driven,' he said. 'He wanted to succeed and he wouldn't be half the performer he is today if he hadn't had that ambition. He was touring, doing panto, doing summer season, and doing thirteen weeks at the London Palladium. He had no time for anybody or anything.'

The marriage was to end amid some degree of bitterness, although in time the two patched things up. Bruce, in later years, was able to display some understanding as to what had gone on. 'It's very difficult in this business when you do hit it and you hit it big, to be a family man, a father, a husband, and a pro. You start drifting apart and all sorts of things happen,' he said. He was also at an age that made it difficult to decide whether to be one thing or another: in this case, the bachelor or the committed family man. Bruce was in his mid-thirties by now, too old to be a skirt-chasing ingénue, and yet not quite middle aged. On the other hand, he had married when he was very young, and quite clearly felt that he'd missed out on a lot. In later years, he was to advise young men to establish themselves before they got married, because otherwise the strains placed on the relationship would be enormous.

In those far off days of discretion and stricter morality, it would have caused a terrible scandal if it were known Bruce was having affairs (indeed, when he eventually ran off with Anthea Redfern some years later, his bosses on *The Generation Game* were horrified). These days, Bruce counters that he and Penny were separated, although they still lived together, when the affairs happened, but they did still take place. 'Let's put it like this,' he said in one interview. 'There are always temptations. Whether you take them or not is up to you. It depends how happy your private life is.' His own private life was anything but happy.

Bruce is not a conquest-lister, but outside his marriages, his most famous liaisons have been with the singer Kathy Kirby and the beauty queen Ann Sidney, who went on to become Miss World in 1964. (This puts Bruce in an extremely elite club: given that his third wife was also a Miss World, he and George Best are the only two men in the world known to have had intimate relations with more than one Miss World. Best, in fact, notched up three.)

Kathy Kirby, also known as Kathy O'Rourke, who bore a slight resemblance to Penny and a stronger one to Marilyn Monroe, was born in Essex in 1940 (or 1938, according to some reports) and, at the age of sixteen began singing for Bert Ambrose and his orchestra. Though he was forty years her senior, Ambrose became her lover and manager, a role he continued until his death in 1971. Kathy continued with his band for three years before striking out on her own. Convent-educated, she could have been an opera singer, and to this day is regarded as one of the greatest voices of her generation.

She also inspired strong feelings in a number of men. 'I have never known anyone with what Kathy had to offer,' Bert said on one occasion, betraying, perhaps, emotions that went rather beyond the professional. 'Voice, tone, range, feeling, personality, and looks. In fact this girl has it all, and nothing can stop her becoming one of the great stars of our time.' That was not quite to be – Kathy's career plummeted after Ambrose's death and she was declared bankrupt before retiring in 1983. In more recent years, her star has been on the rise again: in fact, these days, she has become something of a cult figure as the extent of her talent has been realised once again.

Kathy was introduced to the worldwide audience when she started appearing on television in the early 1960s, and it was here that she also met Bruce. He was not, in fact, her only famous lover – another was Tom

Jones – but her relationship with him enraged Ambrose so much that the two had to meet in secret. Many years later, Bruce admitted the two had been an item: at the time it was kept strictly under wraps.

But it was his other relationship in the early 1960s that attracted most of the attention, with rumours flying even at the time that something was afoot. It also represented something of a recurring theme in Bruce's life. Beauty pageants were to play quite a role where he was concerned, supplying him with one lover, two wives, and general entertainment in both his private and professional life for years to come. At times it seemed that whenever Bruce had a moment off, he was to be found judging a beauty pageant – and in some cases the repercussions, often positive, were to continue for years.

Ann Sidney, who went on to become Miss World, was with Bruce for some time. Born in 1944 in Chippenham, Wiltshire, Ann was to see Miss World as a step out of a slightly difficult existence. Her father was ill after the war and unable to work for some time, and on top of this, rationing was still in place. She clearly hankered for the bright lights of the big city.

'I had a good upbringing, but it was a very simple upbringing,' said Ann in an interview with *The Observer* in 2001, to mark the fiftieth anniversary of Miss World. 'Very working class – my mother was a waitress, and my father worked for a wholesale meat company. So for me, at nineteen, to win the Miss World was a phenomenal experience, and a big, big change.' Ann was to end up with quite a career in her own right, all of it down to stepping on to the beauty pageant stage.

Not that her family had been expecting such a move. Ann was fifteen when she decided she wanted to be a model. Her straightlaced parents – the family was now living in Poole, Dorset – wouldn't hear of it, and so instead had her train as a hairdresser in Bournemouth. This did not, however, work to change Ann's mind. While she was at the hairdresser's, she enrolled for the Bournemouth Regatta Queen to help publicise the salon (and lied about her age, as you had to be sixteen to enter), which she won. A string of beauty contests followed until, in August 1964, she was named Bournemouth's Miss Front Page. She was taken to a ball afterwards to celebrate – and there was Bruce.

Bruce set off in hot pursuit the moment he laid eyes on her. Constantly at her side during the evening, he got her telephone number and took her out to dinner the very next night, telling her he was separated from Penny.

After that came a non-stop bombardment of gifts and notes – using jokey names such as Fred Nurg and Charlie Forthright – which Ann, rather naïvely, allowed to continue. She, meanwhile, had left the beauty salon and won a further series of contests, culminating in Miss United Kingdom, which automatically qualified her to compete in Miss World.

It was then that the first real whiff of scandal struck. Ann flew back to Hurn airport, where amongst the crowd of well-wishers, there was Bruce. He stepped forward, kissed her, murmured 'Well done, darling', and the photo appeared in all the papers, alongside stories of an affair. At that stage, according to all the parties involved, the affair hadn't actually begun. It did not stop Ann's livid father from demanding, 'Have you slept with Bruce Forsyth?' 'No, no, no!' cried Ann and, satisfied with her answer, he let her be.

Penny, on the other hand, was not so easy to convince. She announced to the newspapers that her marriage to Bruce was over; Bruce, anxious to calm down the situation with the woman who had still not actually become his lover, arrived at Ann's parental home. There was no affair, he said, before adding that his marriage really was in trouble. 'He's a real gentleman,' said Ann's father, although that was not a view he was to continue to hold.

With Miss World looming in the distance, Ann moved to a flat in Putney in southwest London, which is when she and Bruce finally did become lovers, not least because at last they had a bit of privacy. After winning Miss World, though, Ann told friends, 'I've lost Bruce now.' For there was not to be a whiff of scandal about Miss Worlds in those days, and not only were they not expected to have affairs with married comedians, but they also were chaperoned heavily to make sure no such thing happened. It made it very difficult to meet. To make matters worse, Ann then signed a £30,000 contract with the International Wool Secretariat, which contained a clause saying that she would be sacked if she were to be found to be misbehaving.

The two, however, were ingenious in their determination to meet. Bruce would get his valet to dress up as a waiter to deliver a bottle of champagne and a note telling her he'd be round later, although even then they were taking a terrible risk. He frequently would arrive at Ann's flat in disguise, once as Columbo, another time with a Hitler moustache, but it couldn't hide the fact that it was really him. One morning the two were, rather foolishly, taking a walk together, with Bruce still in disguise: 'Come off it, Bruce!' bellowed a neighbour, leaning out of a nearby flat window. 'You can't fool us! We'd know that walk anywhere!' Another time, also in disguise, he was crawling through an open window into the flat when the window fell, trapping him. Bruce didn't dare call for help.

And so it went on, although it seems very likely that Bruce was seeing it mainly as a bit of fun. Ann felt that it was her status as Miss World that was putting a dampener on the relationship, but if truth were told, Bruce was giving no real indication that he was prepared to leave Penny for good. When Ann went off on a trip to Australia as part of her duties for the International Wool Secretariat, she came to her senses and, on her return, ended the relationship. Bruce accused her of having met another man: 'No, no!' cried Ann. 'There is no one at all.'

The affair did end for a short time, but two months later Bruce got back in touch. He had moved into a flat in St John's Wood in north London: it looked as if his marriage really was over for good. Ann started seeing him again in secret for the best part of a year, but still Bruce refused to go public, citing the damage it would do to his career. Eventually, the two went on a trip to South Africa together – flying out separately – and she confronted

Bruce about his intentions. He would not marry her, he said, but would like them to go on as they had been doing. Ann took an overdose of sleeping pills, and although she fully recovered, that, finally, was that.

Following the overdose, Ann returned to England, still pursued by cards and love letters from Bruce, but this time there was no going back. Much later, Ann discovered her father had been in touch with Bruce and said that if he really loved Ann, he'd leave her alone. Bruce did.

By the time she gave her interview to *The Observer*, Ann was living in Los Angeles, where she worked as an actress, singer, and dancer. She looked back on it all in a very different light. 'It sounds daft to make an analogy with boxing, about people getting out of their environment or escaping what their destiny was,' she said, 'but to a certain degree, Miss World was something that enabled me financially to go and do something else, instead of saying that my destiny was to not get any further education, to marry, to have children, and stay within the same society that was expected of me. I'm not blaming my parents – it's just how we were then. Now we have many more choices.'

'I would love to have got a further education at that

point, but I feel that in lots of ways the Miss World was a tremendous education for me. I was extremely naïve; in fact I think I'd only been to the Isle of Wight. When I won the Miss World contest, I found myself on the Bob Hope show, flying to Vietnam. My first trip was to LA, and I was picked up in the limousine that the Beatles had used – there were kids still screaming and chasing the limousine. And it wasn't just show business: in Vietnam we would see eighteen-year-old men with their legs blown off. You saw what war could do to people. We've changed – women have changed, everything's changed. And change is good.' There was no mention of Bruce.

In the wake of the affair with Ann, there was no one serious on the horizon, a state of play that was to continue until he met his second wife, Anthea Redfern. Nor were his living arrangements entirely clear. As far as the public was concerned, he was married to Penny, with whom he had three children, with the odd little hiccup along the way. In reality, he moved in and out a few times in a bid for reconciliation, but it never ultimately worked. Penny might have hoped that her husband would eventually return full time, but their lives were just too different now and so were their personalities.

The real fact of the matter was that until he met

Wilnelia – and he was in his fifties when that happened – Bruce was always going to put his work first. He was an utterly driven professional, who had fought like a tiger to get to a preeminent place in the show business jungle, and had no intention of letting anything else, including marriage, get in his way. His affairs were not a sign of a man who deliberately wanted to cheat on his partner, but of a man who was not able, at that time, to put his family at the centre of his life. And, of course, it would be foolish to deny that he liked the attention. No healthy, heterosexual man in their thirties is going to object if a woman throws herself at him, and if Bruce had a few flaws, he was far from being alone. He knew what he wanted and having got it he wasn't going to let go. For all his cavorting with Kathy and Ann, Bruce's real love affair was with work.

He was about to branch out again, to see if he could extend his career in still different directions by making it in another way as a professional on the stage. For Bruce still entertained the desire to be seen as a serious actor, not just a song-and-dance man who could hoof it up with the best of them, but a dramatic player in his own right. It was not to be.

Over the next decade or so, he was to make various

appearances in various roles on stage and screen, some-times to great acclaim. The fact that Bruce never really made it as an actor had nothing to do with his ability. It was more about that most elusive of theatrical help-mates: luck. He was also to come within a cat's whisker of landing some of the most famous roles in the last few decades of film, but, to his continuing anguish, it never quite happened. Bruce had made his breakthrough on a variety programme in television, not as a serious actor. And there, to his obvious chagrin, was where the British public (or at least the casting agents within it) were going to make sure he stayed.

Little Bruce

BRUCE'S PERSONAL LIFE might have been up in the air, but on a professional level he was going as strongly as ever. In 1964, the year Ann Sidney became Miss World, Bruce appeared at the famous cabaret venue, The Talk of the Town, something of a personal risk; if he failed, it could have had a very negative impact on his growing reputation as a performer. He was an established television show host, but could he carry off a couple of hours on stage all by himself? The answer was yes. He was a resounding success. 'It was wonderful,' he said at the time. 'A few months ago, if someone told me I'd be a hit at The Talk of the Town, I'd have had my doubts. But now it's another hurdle I've leaped over. We did wonderful business at the box office.'

His professional aspirations did not stop there. The Talk of the Town had been a challenge, but it was what his long training in variety had prepared him for. Acting was not. But that, increasingly, was where Bruce saw his future: as an actor who could also sing and dance – something akin, in fact, to his heroes Fred Astaire and Sammy Davis Jr.. Both were primarily dancers (and in Sammy's case, also a singer), but both, particularly Astaire, had used their talent to build up spectacular movie careers. Bruce decided to see if he could do it, too.

When the moment came, Bruce took something of a gamble, as he prepared to appear in a musical, *Little Me*, a Neil Simon play that had been a bit on Broadway and was now coming to London. It was quite a departure from what he had been doing, but it catered to one of his strengths: his ability to sing. He was also required to play multiple roles, which meant he'd have a chance to show off his acting range. It was a very big break from the past, but if he wanted to make it as an actor, it had to be done. 'This step you're talking about is essential,' he told one interviewer at the time. 'The chances are that I could have stayed in the kind of thing I've been doing for a few more years. But in show business you can't stand still. So I had to take on a fresh kind of challenge.' This was his chance to show what he could do, and he was determined to give it a go.

The play itself came about because of a meeting a few months previously. 'Early this year, I was rehearsing a sketch with the company of the musical success *How to Succeed in Business Without Really Trying,*' Bruce recalled. 'An impresario tapped me on the back and said, "How would you like to star in a musical? If I bring you a script will you read it?"' A day later the Forsyths were on a plane – and this in the days where it was far less common to use planes as a form of public transport.

'The show had ended its long Broadway run and was on tour, so Penny and I made up our minds to catch it in Detroit,' Bruce explained. 'We decided at midday on a Monday. That evening, we were actually on a plane to New York. On the Tuesday we flew to Detroit, got back to New York on the Wednesday, and we were home in London on the Thursday. I can honestly say I was a bag of nerves on the evening I saw the show.'

But he was convinced, and decided to take on the part. 'It's the story of the men in a rich girl's life,' he continued. 'I play all her lovers – from a sixteen-year-old boy to an eighty-eight-year-old man. Five of the parts I saw myself in quite naturally. The other two, I decided I'd have to work on. It's something of a tour de force. Or you could say a tour de Forsyth.' It also marked the start of the highly successful collaboration between Cy Coleman and the choreographer Bob Fosse; it was not, alas, the start of a huge career for Bruce on the stage.

But he wasn't just doing the play. He continued to appear at The Talk of the Town, continued to tour around the country, continued to work at breakneck speed. The only thing he wasn't doing was appearing on *Sunday Night*... but even there, he was destined to return for the odd one-off show in the future. The pace seemed relentless, but Bruce was adamant he was learning to calm down. 'What's the use of success if you can't enjoy it?' he asked. 'I've a busy time ahead, but I have more control over things. I want to know if I can do a musical, so I have to give up something else – in this case, the *Palladium* spot. I decided that if you have to drive yourself into an early grave in order to be a star, then I'd rather not be a star. From the moment I reached that decision, life has been great. I've found that if you give it a little thought you can still hold the reins and enjoy yourself.'

Wise words, but Bruce really was not ready to adhere to them ... at least for a couple of decades. He might have been able to take the odd holiday and relax a little more, but he remained an utterly driven man, determined to forge ahead with his career. Cabaret, musicals – these were hardly the decisions of a man about to take a back seat. Eventually, though, they took their toll, with Bruce becoming quite seriously ill in the early Sixties.

Norman Wisdom, Bruce Forsyth, and Val Parnell (the man credited with giving Bruce his first big break with *Sunday Night at the London Palladium*) enjoy a cigar and a laugh, c. 1961

1964: *Sunday Night at the London Palladium*, and Bruce introduces perhaps the most influential group in music history, The Beatles.

Bruce with his first wife, Penny Calvert, and their first
two daughters, Debbie and Julie. Cracks were already
beginning to appear in the marriage at this stage.

Bruce had a number of affairs during his marriage to Penny. His affair with Ann Sidney (left), who became Miss World in 1964, ended with her overdosing on pills. He also had a relationship with the singer Kathy Kirby (bottom), who bore some resemblance to his wife.

Bruce performs alongside Beryl Reid (left) and Julie Andrews (right) in the 1968 film flop, *Star!* Despite positive reviews for his role, the film itself was widely panned by critics, and was said to lead to a slump in Andrews's film career.

Bruce's second marriage, to Anthea Redfern, didn't last as long as his first marriage, though the split was more amicable. They are photographed here with the two daughters Bruce and Anthea had together: Charlotte and Louisa.

Bruce poses with Juliet Prowse in 1978 in a
promotional photo for *Bruce Forsyth's Big Night*.
While the show was initially successful, ratings
decreased rapidly, and it lasted only twelve episodes
before being axed.

Bruce had a long-standing friendship with Sammy Davis Jnr., and was one of his greatest admirers. They appeared several times together, and always enjoyed a great rapport on stage.

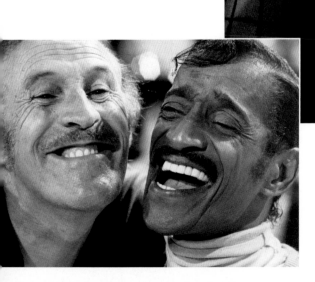

As Bruce became increasingly wealthy, so he became
more extravagant in his material purchases. He
poses here with his Rolls Royce with its personalised
number plate, "BFE": Bruce Forsyth Entertainer.

This illness, which seemed to be some sort of viral infection, came at a tumultuous time in Bruce's life and may well have been caused by all the stress he was under. The strain of working constantly had no doubt taken its toll, for, while Bruce might have been the ultimate professional, even he had his limits. During his illness, he was actually forced to take some time off work – something that was almost unprecedented and has rarely happened since – and attracted some alarmist talk in the media. Ultimately, after a period of very unwilling rest, he made a full recovery.

And then, of course, there was his personal life. His marriage to Penny was over in all but name, but the situation between the two of them was very sour, adding to the stress Bruce felt. He was concerned about maintaining a good relationship with his daughters, but his relationship with his first wife was very bad indeed. It is not difficult to see why Penny might have felt aggrieved. She had, after all, put her career on hold for her marriage, only to see it collapse when her husband hit the big time, a common enough scenario, but distressing nonetheless.

Little Me, originally a 1961 novel by *Auntie Mamie* author Patrick Dennis, had a long run at the Cambridge Theatre, and was a great success. Bruce played opposite

Eileen Gourlay, who took on the role of Belle Poitrine (French for 'beautiful bosom'), and Avril Angers. It was the spoof of a celebrity biography, charting the rise of Belle – who had only two outstanding talents – from poverty to fame and wealth: the original production on Broadway had starred Sid Caesar, taking on all seven of the male roles, while Bruce did the same in the UK.

Bruce was right for the multiple roles for many reasons, not least because, as it has often been observed, *Little Me* is not so much a dramatic play (or musical) as a sketch show. The various roles he was required to undertake included Amos Pinchley, an eighty-something banker who was also colossally mean; Val du Val, a French torch singer; Fred Poitrine, a World War One soldier; Otto Schnitzler, a holiday director; Prince Cherney, the poor ruler of a small European country; and the father and son combo, Noble Eggleston and Noble Jr. Both are highly overachieving men (Noble Snr. goes to Yale and Harvard, becomes a doctor, a lawyer, and a World War One pilot before becoming a successful politician), and the elder of the two is Belle's first love.

Bruce went on to call it, 'the best thing I ever did'. He was not alone in that assessment. There are plenty of critics today who remember it still and have praised his performance. At the time, it must have seemed as if it would lead to fresh dramatic glories and a whole new shape to his career. But, although Bruce was to carry on in acting roles until the 1980s, it was and still remains the highlight of his acting career.

A recording was made of the show and it, too, delighted its audience. 'This is an excellent version of a pretty good show,' ran one review. 'The leads, Bruce Forsyth, Eileen Gourlay, and the wonderful Avril Angers, are streets ahead of Sid Caesar and the Broadway cast. Forsyth is very versatile.' Bruce was widely felt to have carried off the role extremely well.

'I've been so lucky being able to do most of the things I've always wanted to do,' he said in an interview nearly a decade later. 'Most of my ambitions have been fulfilled. Now I enjoy the television shows and the contests, but I love doing cabaret and being an "entertainer" for live audiences. *Little Me* in the West End proved to me that I could act, and I loved that. I've done odd bits of films, but I would, if the right one came along, like to do a big film. That's something to think about for the future.'

In actual fact, on the back of the success of Little Me, ATV gave him his own variety series, The Bruce Forsyth Show, which aired in 1966: the theme tune went, 'I know where I'm going, no more doubts and fears'. In actual fact, this was to prove a little overoptimistic, even though guests included Tom Jones and Douglas Fairbanks Jr., and men of the calibre of Ronnie Corbett and Arthur Mullard took supporting roles. One of the oddities of Bruce's career is that even after he made first his breakthrough and then one comeback after another, there were curiously fallow periods where he had a much lower profile than he was used to. He was about to embark on one of them.

But back then, a new stage career seemed assured. *Little Me* was not his only success (although it was his biggest): he also continued to appear on stage in plays such as *Birds on the Wing*, in which he took over a role played by Ian Carmichael. He also took on a number of roles in television shows. These included the part of Sir Simon de Canterville in *The Canterville Ghost* in 1966 and George Pepper in *Red Peppers*, which was written by Noel Coward, in 1969.

The Astaire/Davis Jr. example was one that Bruce clearly wanted to follow in other ways, too. Both men had forged film careers on the back of their dancing, but Sammy Davis Jr. had also had an equally illustrious career as exactly the sort of performer that Bruce was, on a Las Vegas-style stage. Bruce wanted to make it as an actor, but he also wanted to be an onstage song-and-dance-man like Sammy – and there's no question that the talent was there. It's difficult to say exactly why this never came about.

Bruce himself put it down to a certain snobbery in British show business circles, to the effect that if you made your mark in one field, it was very difficult to move to another, and there was almost certainly something in that. For, while 'Beat the Clock' had been a hugely popular part of *Sunday Night…*, it was not until the 1970s that Bruce became so utterly identified with game shows that it was sometimes forgotten he could do anything else. Back in the 1960s, he did get plenty of chances to prove himself, and it appears that what really held him back was simply bad luck. A couple of the choices he made were questionable, though there was no doubt he was an extremely talented song-and-dance man.

In television terms, these were actually rather difficult years. Looking back, Bruce believes it might have been for the best, forcing him back onto the stage for one-man shows and making him hone his craft even more. 'They were lean times, but very important for me,' he said. 'By working clubs, I started to establish a longer act. Before then, although I could do all the things I do – play the piano, sing, dance, impressions – I didn't have a long act. Sammy Davis Jr. had been over and he went on and did an hour-and-a-half. What I was learning was how to extend it and pace it. It meant that after *The Generation Game* I could do the one-man show that has been such a success at the Palladium – go on with a nice, big orchestra, and do two, two-and-a-half hours on my own.'

He also went on to play in quite a number of films, an aspect of his career that has now been largely forgotten. None of these films were quite the hits he had hoped for, but Bruce himself is the first to concede that that's show business. If they had been massive successes, Bruce might well have ended up as a movie star.

The first of these, in 1968, was *Star!*, a film about the life of Gertrude Lawrence, with Julie Andrews playing the title role. Bruce was Arthur Lawrence, her father. The film was not a success: some believe it actually contributed to the decline of the film musical, while also damaging Julie Andrews's career.

Ironically, it was Julie's huge earlier success in *The Sound of Music* that had led to the film being made in the first place. Twentieth Century Fox had wanted to replicate the earlier hit, and so alongside *Star!*, also produced *Hello Dolly* and *Dr Doolittle*. None of them did particularly well, although in fairness, audience tastes were changing. Musicals were not as popular as they once were.

However, its length – nearly three hours – and (in the eyes of some critics) lack of plot didn't help. Bruce acquitted himself perfectly well, but couldn't do a great deal against the background of the wider problems on the film. *Halliwell's Film Guide* summed it up. 'Elephantiasis finally ruins this patient, likeable recreation of a past theatrical era,' it reported. 'In the old Hollywood style, it would probably have been even better on a smaller budget; but alas the star would still have been ill at ease with the drunken termagant scenes.'

Next up were *Can Hieronymous Merkin Ever Forget Mercy Humppe* and *Find True Happiness* in 1969. Co-written and directed by its star Anthony Newley, and also featuring Newley's then wife Joan Collins, this was an eccentric 1960s vehicle, which, in some eyes, is now a cult classic – but not, it must be said, in very many eyes. This was, perhaps, Bruce's worst choice of anything he appeared in, although again, that was not exactly his fault. Anthony Newley, at that time a massively popular and bankable star, had been allowed far too much of a free hand in the making of this vanity vehicle, the result being a bloated, silly, pretentious mess, with almost no redeeming feature at all.

'If I'd been Anthony Newley, I would have opened it in Siberia during Christmas week and called it a day,' observed the critic Rex Reed, while Michael Billington wrote, 'The kindest thing for all concerned would be that every available copy should be quietly and decently buried.' It was an episode best forgotten by all, which, given that copies of the film still exist, has not entirely happened. Fortunately for him, most people have no idea that this was a farrago in which Bruce had any part.

The Julie Andrews connection reared its head again in Bruce's next film, *Bedknobs and Broomsticks*, which was Disney's belated follow-up to *Mary Poppins*, but had nothing like the same success. Starring Angela Lansbury and David Tomlinson – who had played Mr Banks in *Mary Poppins* – and set in 1940, it is the story of a witch and three children who are evacuated to the country during the war, and who fly around on a magic bedstead, saving England. Bruce played a character called Swinburne.

Roger Ebert, of the *Chicago Sun-Times*, wrote a review that very much summarised the widespread opinion. '*Bedknobs and Broomsticks* is the new Disney production from the team that made *Mary Poppins*, and it has the same technical skill and professional polish,' he said. 'It doesn't have much of a heart, though, and toward the end you wonder why the *Poppins* team thought kids would like it much. They sit still for part of it; they like the fly-ing bed and the scenes with animated animals, and when the empty suits of armor attack the Nazis there's a kind of *Creature Features* enjoyment. But what are Nazis do-ing in this picture, anyway? And why is it necessary for a character to exclaim, toward the end of the movie: "We have driven the Hun into the sea"?' Despite not living up to expectations, it was not, however, on the same scale of awfulness as the Anthony Newley vehicle, and it is still viewed with some fondness by viewers today.

There then followed yet another ill-advised outing in 1971 in *The Magnificent Seven Deadly Sins*, directed and produced by Graham Stark. Now largely, and some would say thankfully, forgotten, the film is made up of seven sketches, each representing a sin, and each written by a member of the British comedy establishment. The film might have worked, for it represented the cream of the British comedy establishment of the day, including Harry Secombe, June Whitfield, Harry H Corbett, Bill Pertwee, Ian Carmichael, Ronnie Barker, and others too numerous to mention.

But it didn't. Bruce took part in the first sketch, 'Avarice', and a brief summary might explain why it failed to take off. Bruce played Clayton, a chauffeur with a rich boss. His boss sees a 50p piece fall into a sewer and makes Clayton go in after it. Various other people become involved in the search, the boss sees sewage on Clayton, fires him, falls into an open sewer, and Clayton replaces the manhole, walking away with the coin. It was an episode best forgotten by everyone who became involved, and, indeed, it has been.

Bruce has, in more recent years, voiced regret that he didn't have more of a film career, but he was very unfortunate in his choice of film. He also lost out on a few parts that might otherwise have made his name in that world, and harbours regrets about it to this day. 'I'd more or less got the part in a film called *Candleshoe*, because David Niven had turned it down,' he said around the time of his eightieth birthday. 'But Niven changed his mind when he found out that Jodie Foster, who was a huge star even as a child, was going to be in it. And Lionel Bart wanted me as Fagin in *Oliver!* when Ron Moody wasn't sure whether to do it, which would have been wonderful for me. Those are two of the biggest letdowns of my life. Those things don't come along every day and they could have made all the difference to my career. They are regrets I will never get over. I still find myself thinking, "Hey, what would have happened if I'd got that part?"' He was also up for the role of the Childcatcher in *Chitty Chitty Bang Bang*, which eventually went to Robert Helpmann.

Bruce was not destined to be a movie star. Although these were not the last dramatic performances he made, his career was about to take a sharp turn in a totally different direction, one that was about to cement his reputation as one of the outstanding entertainers of his day. Does he mind? The evidence is that he does. But he was to be very handsomely rewarded – and recognised for his talent – elsewhere.

Meanwhile, his marriage really was falling apart. As far back as 1964, Penny had declared, 'Bruce and I are finished. He is a great guy, but things have not gone well between us for some time. There's no hope of a reconciliation.' They did, in fact, talk about it from time to time, and in 1967 there were reports they were trying to make another go of it, but it all came to nothing, and in 1968, Penny again declared that it was over. 'We have been separated for two months [sic] and now I'm starting divorce proceedings,' she said. 'The reconciliation just didn't work out. I'm not blaming anyone or anything. It's just one of those things. I have known Bruce for twenty years. We met when we were doing a Windmill show together. Now I shall have to learn to live without him all over again.' In actual fact, the divorce was not to come through for another five years – the same year Bruce married his second wife, Anthea Redfern. It was to cause a good deal of grief.

Bruce himself was rather ambivalent about it all. 'In the past six years, we have been separated for at least four, and I suppose things will finally be resolved,' he said in an interview in 1970 with the *Sunday Express*. He was right.

Many years later, in 1987, in his mid-fifties, when he was very happily married to his third wife Wilnelia, Bruce was able to accept that he had been at fault. Nothing was going to be allowed to interfere with his career back then (including other love affairs), and nothing did. 'It was very difficult then,' he said. 'Thirty years ago, I was getting my act together, rehearsing, performing, travelling. I was away almost constantly touring and that puts a great strain on a relationship. I'm sure I was very difficult to live with, simply because I wasn't there and everything was geared towards work rather than home.' Penny would

certainly have agreed with him; the break-up, the rec-
onciliations, and finally the divorce caused wounds that
took decades to heal.

The fallow patch continued for him as far as television was concerned. He appeared from time to time, but
in the late 1960s there still wasn't a Bruce vehicle running full time. Did this disappoint him? 'No,' he told the
Sunday Express. 'I think it's good for the public to have
a rest from me, and it's good for me to have a rest from
television. I've been offered my own TV shows, but I ask
myself: "What kind of show can I do?" I don't want to do
something for the sake of doing it. I want to come back
to television with a different kind of show; with a slightly
new kind of Bruce.' Later he admitted he'd been putting
a brave face on it, but no matter. The good times were to
start to roll again soon enough.

He was also aware of the perils of overdoing it. 'For
the first few years after becoming known on television,
I worked very hard,' he continued. 'I had waited a good
many years for success and I had to consolidate it. But if
you work like that, you have to take the consequences. I
went for a check-up the other day and I was told I was
in great shape. I'll tell you something that pleased me. A
nurse was taking some tests and she said, "Now relax". A

few minutes later she said, "You're a good relaxer". I told her, "Maybe I've had to learn how to do it."'

'Nowadays I don't overwork any more. I recently recorded the *Gracie Fields' Christmas Show* and the *Rolf Harris Show* in a week. That was the hardest week's work I've done this year. There was a time when I was working that hard, and harder, all the time. Now I take the opportunity to be out of work. When I'm doing late night cabaret, for example, I usually go to bed for at least an hour in the evening. If I don't do that, I flake out on the floor of the dressing room. I've developed the ability to relax for short periods. Once that would have been impossible.'

He was, indeed, sounding quite unlike the manic Bruce of yesteryear, leading the paper to ask if he'd given up his ambition. 'My big ambition now is to become an international act,' declared Bruce. 'I don't want to leave this country – it's still the only place to live – but I do feel I'm ready to spread my wings.'

It was not an ambition he was ever going to achieve. Just around the corner lurked the vehicle that was to boost Bruce's fame in Britain even further, affording him the greatest success of an astonishing career to date. It was *The Generation Game*.

Give Us A Twirl

THE GENERATION GAME – or *Bruce Forsyth and the Generation Game* as it was called when it was first broadcast in 1971 – was based on a Dutch television show called *Een van de acht*, or 'one of the eight', a format first put together by Mies Bouwman, a popular Dutch talk show host. Game shows were becoming an increasingly popular staple of British television – not least because they were considerably cheaper to produce than variety shows – and the hosts of variety shows were being recruited to make the leap into game shows. There was no contest as to who the king of the variety show was; Bruce was a shoe-in for the job.

The game had eight competitors – 'Let's meet the eight who are going to generate' – and in the first two rounds, two couples would compete against each other, at the end of which the couple with the lowest score would be eliminated. The games usually involved the couples watching a professional doing something expertly – such as pottery or dancing – and then trying, amidst much hilarity, to do the same. The other game would take the nature of a quiz.

The two highest scoring couples made it through to the final, which tended to be a big set-piece number, such as a drama or farce. The winners would make it through to the conveyor belt, where they would win as many items (dinner services, fondue sets, toys) as they could remember. There were also 'Brucie Bonuses', seemingly worthless items, which would then open up to reveal a holiday.

It was to be one of the greatest successes of Bruce's career, proving incredibly popular with audiences and viewers alike. It was to introduce some of Bruce's most famous catchphrases, most notably, 'Didn't he do well,' and, of course, 'Nice to see you, to see you...' 'Nice!' the ecstatic audience would reply. There was also, 'Let's have a look at the jolly old score board'. Later, when the show was revived and Bruce's assistant was Rosemarie Ford, this changed to, 'What's on the board, Miss Ford?' It was the show when Bruce first postured in his 'strong man' pose – a pose that, along with some of those catchphrases, he retains to this day and, of course, it was to introduce him to the woman who would become his second wife, Anthea Redfern. All in all, it made quite a change to his life.

It was not just the fact that Bruce was the biggest name in variety television that made him so right for the job: it was the fact that he was able to handle an audience so well. The participants on *The Generation Game* were, to put it bluntly, required to make idiots of themselves, which meant that they had to be handled with extreme care. They needed a host who could tease them without ever going over the top. Bruce was that man.

It was also Bruce who was responsible for the way the show was staged, which undoubtedly contributed to its enormous success. 'Forget it's television: think of it as a stage show,' he said to the technicians. Unusually, he asked for the first few rows to be lit, so that he could see the audience's faces. 'I like to see who's getting ready to leave,' he teased. 'Harry Secombe was the opposite. He used to tell me he preferred it in darkness. He couldn't see them anyway because he had bad eyesight.'

Funnily enough, in the glory years of the programme, when it was playing on Saturday nights at 5.45pm on BBC1, Bruce was, in effect, the warm-up man for the programmes to come after it, most notably *Morecombe and Wise*. It was exactly the same role that he'd played all those years previously in variety, and he wasn't thrilled about it at the time. In later years, though, he began to appreciate his position. '*Doctor Who, The Generation Game, The Duchess of Duke Street, Morecambe and Wise, Parkinson,*' he recalled. 'I used to moan about it. I'm a good moaner. You'll never find anyone better at moaning than me. "Why are we on at 5.45, for goodness sake?" I'd ask. "Why can't we be on at seven?" But I always know when I'm wrong, and I was wrong. I was The Hook.'

A great deal that was phenomenally popular on the show came about by chance, not least the famous 'strong man' pose. It actually happened because Bruce was larking around. 'It was 1971, and we were rehearsing for the first series of *The Generation Game,*' he recalled. 'We were running through the opening of the show and the producer told me to just stand at the back of the stage and wait for the spotlight. I thought, "I can't just stand there like an idiot". So I did that pose and everyone laughed. The producer loved it and told me to keep it in.'

The famous catchphrase, meanwhile, actually already existed, but it was during *The Generation Game* that it finally got a grip on the nation, which is where it stayed. Asked where it came from, Bruce replied, 'I coined it. I'd used it on TV in the 1960s and then I did a commercial for the *TV Times* where a guy came up to me in a pub and said, "It is you, isn't it? Nice to see you, to see you nice". After that, people started shouting it at me on the street. People love it because you can say it to anybody.'

Once the show began, Bruce never actually met the contestants until the cameras were rolling, and had about a minute to put them at their ease. He managed it with aplomb. There would be a brief run through of their name, occupation, and interests, at the end of which even the most terrified would be relaxed. 'After that, they'll do anything,' said Bruce.

Another secret of his success was that, unless someone was being a bit obnoxious, Bruce always remained very sympathetic to the people appearing on the show. 'Everyone likes to see ordinary people having a go,' he said, and he always ensured matters never got out of hand. In fact, an atmosphere of mild anarchy was much in evidence, although again, that was appearance rather than reality. Bruce always knew exactly what he was doing: there was never a chance he'd lose control.

Very ironically, in later years Bruce began to feel that it was shows such as *The Generation Game* that actually killed off variety television. 'Variety suffered as people shows took over, and *The Generation Game* was the first people show. Everything that's happened since has been a spin-off from *The Generation Game*,' he said, and he may well be right. It might be stretching it to call *The Generation Game* reality television, but it did make stars of some of the contestants, briefly at least.

What preoccupied Bruce most to begin with was his hostess. It has often been assumed that Bruce and Anthea met when he was hosting *The Generation Game*: that is not quite right. In actual fact, Anthea was compering a Lovely Legs beauty contest at which Bruce was a judge. At the same time, he was looking for a hostess to work with him on his new show. By the time he met Anthea, fifty-two women had already auditioned, but the chemistry wasn't there with any of them. Bruce, however, clearly sensed the potential and asked Anthea to audition. She got the job. This, ultimately, led to another famous catchphrase: 'Give us a twirl!'

Anthea, a gentle woman, was in many ways very different from the image she portrayed. Tall, blonde, and slim, she was an extremely eye-catching young woman, with something of a scarred background. She might have ended up as a beauty, but it certainly wasn't there in her childhood. 'I was so skinny and incredibly unattractive as a child that people would say to my mother: "Isn't she plain? Isn't she thin? Whatever is she going to do in life?"' she recalled. 'My mother would reply: "Don't worry, she will grow from an ugly duckling into a beautiful swan." I don't think they meant to be cruel, but I was aware of it and I think that's why I wanted to be a model.'

Anthea had two younger sisters, Lisa and Trudy; home was in Torquay. But there was insecurity about her childhood. Her gambling addict father started as a grocer, but then became a bookmaker, to his own delight and to the family's chagrin. 'He did lose large sums, but he was still able to afford to send us all to private schools,' said Anthea. 'I know my mother got very worried at times. One day he would come home in a new Jaguar and the next month he'd be in a Volkswagen. He would tell my mother he had not been happy with the way the Jag was running and she'd look at me as if to say: "Oh yes, how much did he lose?"'

Anthea's mother played a huge role in establishing her daughter's confidence. Anthea grew into a tall teenager, and it was her mother who said, 'With your height, you'll make a beautiful model.' She was right. 'It was my mother who was the pusher behind me,' Anthea recalled. 'She gave me the confidence to take a modelling course

– and when I got a job at Christian Dior in Paris, I felt like the ugly duckling who becomes a swan.'

As with Bruce, this was actually Anthea's second marriage. She was with her first husband – a professional footballer with Torquay United called Robin Stubbs – for only ten months. She was only seventeen. 'When he asked me to marry him, I was so flattered and overwhelmed that I just didn't think about being too young to take on the responsibility of marriage,' she confessed. 'Neither of us realised that you have to work at a marriage – not just sit back and hope it works out, which is what I did. But when we split up, we were still friends.' She was quite irritated when this came up in the run-up to her marriage to Bruce: 'Well, these things happen, don't they?' she said. 'I was only seventeen, far too young, and I got married partly as a gesture of independence.'

She resumed her modelling career, moving to London, where she became Miss London, before ending up on *The Generation Game*. Anthea was twenty-three, Bruce was forty-five, and she was adamant that the age gap would make no difference. 'People often ask about the twenty years that separate Bruce and me,' she said defiantly, after they were married. '"What about age?" they say. "Does that worry you?" I tell them, "Yes, mine does". Not that

I worry about losing my looks, because everyone grows to look older. But I never want to grow old mentally. If I did that, I'd feel much older than Bruce, because he will always stay young at heart.'

This, then, was the woman who was to become Bruce's second wife: a gentle people-pleaser who'd grown up with an unreliable man as a father. Like Bruce, when the relationship finally ended some years down the line, she married again, but the two remained on good terms.

Back then, Bruce was entranced and it wasn't long before the relationship became more than professional. 'The moment I knew I'd fallen in love with him was when he came into my dressing room,' Anthea recalled years later. 'I was sitting there in Carmen rollers but no makeup and he kissed me. I remember thinking: "I wanted to be glamorous when he first kissed me." But he didn't mind. I just thought of him as a lovely man who was a tower of strength.' Indeed, she was besotted. 'I blushed furiously through all that cream,' she recalled. 'There was the star of the show, wanting to kiss me – and I was as embarrassed as any gangling school kid.'

Although he was technically still married to Penny, the two had been separated for some years and Bruce, typically, had quite a number of women going at the time. Although she was later painted as a marriage wrecker, Anthea was keen to explain that, in reality, the situation was quite different. 'In fact, when I met him, he was juggling four very beautiful girlfriends so I certainly wasn't the cause of the break-up of his marriage,' she said. 'Penny wasn't always complimentary about us, and I understand the meaning of the saying: "Hell hath no fury like a woman scorned". Some women can't handle it, and I don't blame them. But if a man is happy in his marriage, even if he does have the odd indiscretion, he will do everything in his power to cover it up. But if he's not happy in a relationship, then it becomes something more than just an odd indiscretion.'

Indeed, Bruce did not try to cover it up. 'When we fell in love, we didn't exactly keep our romance a secret,' Anthea recalled. 'So when an English journalist spotted me with Bruce when he toured Canada, he told Bruce, "Either I write a nasty story about you being here with the hostess of your TV show, or you tell me the truth". Bruce said to me, "To hell with it, I have nothing to hide. I love you and I want to marry you. I don't care who knows it". When the story first hit the headlines, Bruce's first wife, Penny, commented, "I'm not surprised. Bruce is always falling in love. I wouldn't be surprised if he didn't fall in love with the Queen next."'

And so the secret was out: Bruce had fallen in love with his glamorous co-presenter. There had been affairs before, but this was different. The couple were serious about one another and wanted to marry. Their romance caused outrage in some quarters, not least with Bruce's bosses at the BBC, who played pretty dirty to try to force Bruce to do what they wanted.

'One day the producers came to the flat,' said Anthea. 'They said: "We want to talk to just you, Bruce". But he said: "Anything you want to say to me you can say in front of Anthea". So I said I would pop out and buy some sugar. While I was out, they told him that, because he was married and we had fallen in love, they couldn't use me any more because of the bad press it would generate. Bruce was just so loyal and wonderful. He said: "If you don't have her, you don't have me". I told him not to be so silly. This was a big break for him and I didn't want to jeopardise it, but he said: "It's not fair. I've been separated all these years and I'll go out with whom I want."'

'So what the BBC did was to bring in four more hostesses for the next show. They were former beauty queens in gorgeous halter-necks. They put me in the frumpiest grey dress, with a frill under my chin. I looked like a choirboy. They wanted to push me into the background and then oust me. But so many people wrote in saying they hadn't seen enough of me that they had to give in.'

That was, indeed, an act of real loyalty on Bruce's part. Given how much he'd sacrificed in previous years for the sake of his career – not least his first marriage – to put his new job on the line was an indication of quite how much he really felt for Anthea. This was no mere fling.

The papers were having a field day. Anthea was portrayed as the scarlet woman, who had run off with someone else's husband after twenty years of marriage. She was, not unnaturally, upset. 'I was made to look like a horrible, painted blonde who stole husbands, and that hurt,' she recalled afterwards. 'I've never met Bruce's first wife, but she looks like an attractive woman from photographs I've seen. And what everyone forgot to mention was that Bruce had left her eight years before he met me, so I didn't split them up. I don't think his wife had been sitting all alone at home crying all those years, just as Bruce had many lovely girl-friends before he met me. The difference was he proved he wanted to marry me by finally getting a divorce.'

In 1973, the year his divorce came through, Bruce and Anthea tied the knot on Christmas Eve. It was a small affair, in front of a dozen relatives at Windsor Register Office. Initially, it seemed as if they'd each found their soulmate. 'To me, half of being in love is being loved in return,' said Anthea, a year after the wedding. 'I've never been the sort of girl who loves hopelessly when the man just isn't interested. But once Bruce told me that he loved me, I didn't need to hold back my emotions any longer. We discovered the reason the other night why we're so happy together. We're such incredibly good friends. We're each other's best mate, and there's nothing we don't confide in each other. He's a terribly romantic person. What I love are the little surprises that he'll spend hours shopping to find for me. Not expensive gifts, but he hides them away and carefully wraps them up to bring out on all the days that mean something special to both of us. There's never a moment in the day when I don't know where he is. If he goes out when I'm not there, I'll come home to find a little love letter waiting for me.'

Bruce had been swept off his feet as much as Anthea had: here, after all, was a blonde, gorgeous girl more than twenty years younger than him, who was also totally devoted to him. At that time, the two were revelling in their relationship with one another. They started their married life living in Bruce's flat in Ascot, but shortly afterwards moved to a house just outside Wentworth golf course in Surrey.

Anthea was an intensely domesticated woman, and so it was Bruce, the elder member of the partnership by two decades, who was always dragging the two of them out on the town. 'It's me who has to say, "Come on, let's go out for dinner tonight",' said Bruce, a couple of years into the marriage. 'She's quite happy to stay at home.' So, often, was he: the pair confessed that they had special nights when they would retire to bed at nine o'clock, with a glass of wine and a snack, to watch the television at the end of the bed. 'We just always seemed to get on well,' Bruce continued, 'and we found ourselves wanting to see each other more and more.'

Now utterly established at the top of his game, Bruce's professionalism never faltered. *The Generation Game* was introducing him to a whole new set of fans, and his self-control remained as iron clad as ever. Anthea might have been running the show at home, but when it came to his work clothes, Bruce insisted on doing all the washing and ironing himself. He would soak his shirts overnight in the basin in his hotel room, when he was out on tour, and use the kettle to get creases out.

He took enormous care of his clothes, another legacy of his sixteen years on the road before he finally made it, when he had only one stage suit. 'I used to see some of the others nipping across the road to the pub, spilling beer all over their stage clothes and I used to think what a waste of suits it was,' he recalled. 'I made it a firm rule that I would never sit down once I had put my stage suit on before a show. I still keep to it. I never sit down in my show suit; it spoils the creases.'

Bruce's career had hardly needed reviving, but with *The Generation Game*, it was taking on a new lease of life. He was constantly invited on to other people's shows, in 1971 appearing on *Cilla* and *The Val Doonican Show*, and in 1972 receiving the ultimate showbiz accolade at the time: an invitation to appear on *The Morecombe and Wise Christmas Show*. (He accepted.) In 1975, he appeared with Frankie Howerd on *Frankie and Bruce*. He was on a roll.

In his private life, Bruce was turning into a slightly more laid-back person than he had been before. 'When people see me perform, they think I look like a person who can never relax,' he told the *TV Times* in 1976. 'But if I sit down, I can turn off the Bruce Forsyth who is the vitamin pill on legs. I couldn't keep that up all the time. I can relax in a car or a chair: close my eyes and go off to another world. Like everybody else, I've had dramas through my life. Not only personal-wise, but drama-wise, business-wise. These things happen. But I've always been a lucky person because I can switch off and work. I'm glad about that because I know some people in our business can't do it. Some can't face an audience with any sort of tension hanging over them. And I sympathise, because it's the only business where you have to put on an act completely different from how you feel.'

Even with that more relaxed attitude, however, Bruce still found it very difficult to take too much time off. The money was irrelevant. 'It doesn't make any difference to how much I earn really,' he said. 'I don't think about money that much. I suppose it's easy to say that, because I've got a few bob, but I haven't really taken a lot of time off. It's the old variety performer in me, I think: if you do have more than two or three weeks off work you get restless feeling that you're never going to work again.'

And he was certainly up for new challenges. In 1976, he returned for one week to his old stomping ground at the London Palladium, with his one-man show. It was certainly taxing: Bruce was on stage for a total of two-and-three-quarter hours, with only a fifteen-minute break: it impressed critics and audiences alike. That week was 'probably the happiest of my life,' said Bruce. 'It's wonderful what *The Generation Game* has done for me. My first audience, from *Sunday Night at the London Palladium*, has grown up and had kids. But this time it was all ages, from elderly people to young people.'

His personal life was going well, too, with Anthea very much building up the family home. The Forsyth's house oozed wealth: a large entrance hall led onto an even larger sitting room, with a bar and swimming pool further on. There were four bedrooms (the master bedroom had two dressing rooms, his and hers) along with staff quarters. They led a fairly quiet life: 'We don't really like big parties,' Anthea explained. 'I think it is far more intimate to have a really nice dinner party. And anyway, I don't want a whole lot of people dropping ash and spilling drinks everywhere just as we've got the house nice.'

Anthea was coming across as the suburban housewife, and in many ways she seemed an ideal mate for Bruce. For a start, she was as nitpicky as he was. 'I think it comes from being married to a perfectionist,' she said at the time. 'When we first got together, do you know, I was never allowed to wash his clothes in case I didn't do it right? He washed everything himself by hand. His shirts had to be drip dried on special hangers with the top button and third button done up, and the collars and cuffs had to be smoothed out with the thumbs in a special way while still wet. When he finally decided to show me how to do it, I remember thinking, "What am I getting involved in?"'

Bruce's perfectionism revealed itself in other ways, not least a hot temper when he was getting worked up before a show. One journalist asked a publicity girl for *The Generation Game* if he could come to watch the show being recorded: 'I don't know how he will react,' she replied. 'He can be very, very difficult, one of those people who controls everything and everybody. On the programme day, no-one is allowed near him. If a journalist tries to speak to him, he will blow his top and then everyone suffers from the fall-out.'

Bruce himself was able to admit that sometimes things could get a little tense. 'I hate incompetence,' he said. 'If I do one little thing wrong in a show, I will be kicking myself afterwards and will make sure I do it right next time. If I lose a laugh, I will try to work out what went wrong and correct it. Lackadaisical people make me angry. If I think someone is not trying hard enough and is incompetent on top, I can't bear it; I would rather not have that person around me. I want him out of my sight.'

Bruce acknowledged that he had been extraordinarily lucky in later years. 'I always think now that even if nothing else happens, I have got lots of things to look back on and be thrilled about, lots of very happy memories. There are plenty of things I still want to do – I'd love a really good part in a film, for example – but if it doesn't happen, well, I think I can honestly say I am probably at the happiest time of my life now. It sounds terrible, doesn't it? But it's true.'

There had been a small amount of tension with his daughters at the time he married Anthea (Bruce had not alerted them in advance, as he wanted to tell them face to face, but a photographer spilled the beans, causing some upset) but matters were much calmer there, too. Indeed, Julie, now seventeen, was following her dad into show business in a group called Guys and Dolls. 'Now they are grown up, I don't have to see them every day of the week to know I am close to them,' said Bruce. 'They are my daughters and I am their dad and nothing will ever change that and that's lovely.' Under the circumstances, it was a happy end.

I Am Quite Anti-Social

ANTHEA WAS HAPPY being the homemaker, but this was, ironically, what was eventually going to force the couple apart. At first, Bruce was happy with this, too. The feminist movement of the 1970s liked to complain that Anthea should have a bigger role on *The Generation Game*. 'They obviously haven't taken into account that Anthea is already cooking, sewing, ironing, and looking after the dogs, as well as bringing me my slippers,' retorted Bruce. 'How on earth can she do any more?'

But this was not, actually, exactly what he wanted: he wanted a woman with whom he could travel the world. Anthea was disinclined to do this by temperament, but she had another two very good reasons to stay at home, too: Charlotte, who was born on 22 December 1976, and Louisa, who arrived on 7 November 1977. Bruce was delighted, but it fundamentally changed the nature of their relationship and, sadly, was the beginning of the end.

Anthea was not born to be a model or game show

hostess: she was born to be a wife and mother. As she herself so often made clear, she preferred domesticity, the hearth and home, and small intimate gatherings to loud showbiz parties – and now that she had children, her focus shifted from Bruce to her girls. No one was at fault and no one was to blame, but the couple's priorities had changed. Bruce adored his little daughters, as he adored all his children, but he still wanted to get out there and travel the world. Anthea did not.

And so cracks began to appear in his second marriage, which was to prove rather shorter than the first. On the outside, all looked well: his television career was going better than ever, and he was preparing to take on new challenges, one of them a brave choice indeed. He was going to be playing a character called Fred Limelight – an entertainer who never quite made it. In other words, the man Bruce so nearly became.

It was 1978. Bruce was getting set to play Manchester's Palace Theatre in a play called *The Travelling Music Show*. It had been touring around the country, prior to a London run, and he was reminiscing about the old days, when he'd been to that very theatre two decades previously. 'Playing second spot is the lowest of the low on any variety bill,' he said. 'I had it in the first half and Norman

Vaughan had it in the second half. The Beverley Sisters were top of the bill, but there was another very funny comic called Freddie Sales, who was absolutely killing the audience. I had a pretty good act at that time, but nobody had heard of me and coming on early, you are supposed to warm the audience up in just ten minutes. It was murder. Norman Vaughan and I used to pass in the corridor and we would just shake our heads at each other. It was always a pretty hard house, this one.'

But now just about everyone had heard of him, and Bruce was taking on a role that could have been written with him in mind. Sporting a moustache, which he was to keep from then on, Bruce was taking on the part of Fred Limelight in a show that was directed by Burt Shevelove, produced by Hillard Elkins, and with a score by Leslie Bricusse. It was a brave choice. Show business is a notoriously superstitious profession, so much so that Sammy Davis Jr. had initially been overly reluctant to sing Mr Bojangles, about an itinerant song-and-dance man for fear that he, too, would end up like that. Bruce could have been forgiven for feeling the same way about Fred Limelight, for he was well aware of the resonance here.

'Fred is a Bruce Forsyth who never made it, the man

I had the fear of becoming,' he said. 'If the break had not happened as it did, it could have happened to me. Fred is a good performer; he is an attacker – like I am. It's just that he is a little bit off, sometimes. He can make contact with the audience. But he does not get the breaks. And that is show business. You fall by the wayside unless the lucky break happens at the right time. Luckily, it happened to me.'

In the many years it took for him to reach the top, he knew exactly the man that Fred Limelight was. 'Fred, to my mind, is a bit "end-of-the-pier" at Clacton,' he said. 'He has to fight the whole of show business: the manager of the theatre, the orchestra, the conductor, and the stage people. It is sink or swim for him. When I turned from song and dance to be a comic I gave myself five years. I'd either make it or not. But I didn't want to be left with sour grapes in my mouth for the rest of my life. I didn't want to be Fred Limelight. In the fifth year, *Palladium* happened.'

Needless to say, Bruce was tackling the role with his typical enthusiasm and professionalism. 'For two months, I have done nothing but eat, drink, and sleep this show,' he said. 'It is like a never-ending jigsaw puzzle. You are always trying to find another piece here, another piece there, to make it better. We have had quite a good morning today. We have come up with a couple of new ideas. One would think it gets easier as you get nearer the first night. But there is still so much to do. There is not a lot of enjoyment in it at this stage except finding the odd good idea. You just want to be left alone and get on with it.'

The show was not a success. It made it to the West End, but folded after only four months, leading some critics to complain that Bruce had made the mistake of thinking that he was bigger than *The Generation Game*. That was, in fact, grossly unfair: given the amount of time he had spent in the business, there was no reason why Bruce shouldn't do well in a West End musical. But it was not to be.

Rather more serious, however, was his greatest television flop. There had been highs and lows in his television work before, but he failed on a scale that was hugely embarrassing for him with 1978's *Bruce Forsyth's Big Night* on ITV. ITV had been desperate to lure him away from the BBC for years, and offered him £15,000 a week, a huge sum in those days, for two hours of prime time viewing on Saturday night. The show itself cost £250,000 to produce: there was to be music, competitions, and pre-recorded items. In other words, it was a variety show

– exactly the type of programme that Bruce later came to believe *The Generation Game* killed off.

At first it seemed to be exactly what Bruce wanted. He had been complaining that his Saturday night slot on the BBC was not quite prime time enough, and this put him in the most prestigious slot of the most popular night for watching television in the week – and this was 1978, when audience figures could reach over twenty million. Anthea was roped in, Jimmy Edwards and Ian Lavender recreated the hit radio show *The Glums*, Charlie Drake did the same for *Worker*, and Steve Jones hosted *The Pyramid Game*. Cannon and Ball also recorded segments for the show, although these were never broadcast (the show did, however, launch the duo). The *TV Times* was certain it was going to be a success: 'You're going to do well, every Saturday night – no dear, it's not Saturday Night Fever. No, I'm not John Travolta. It's *Bruce Forsyth's Big Night*.'

It didn't work. Initially it brought in high ratings, the biggest ever for London's LWT, but it simply couldn't compete with a show on the other channel – *The Generation Game*. Larry Grayson had taken over from Bruce and was proving to be as much up to the job as Bruce had been, garnering a huge following. Perhaps the new show was too overblown, perhaps the appetite for this kind of show was no longer there, but the ratings slipped down the plughole, and the show did not last long. Used to success with everything he touched, Bruce behaved much like a wounded animal, blaming the press and much else besides. Even at his stage of the game, this was a crushing disappointment, and one he could hardly bear.

Worse was to come. It had long been Bruce's dream to crack Broadway, and in 1979 it seemed as if that, too, might be happening, when he was booked to appear at the Winter Garden Theatre. His old pals turned out in force: Sammy Davis Jr. was there, as was Anthony Newley, Millicent Martin, and David Frost. The audience was actually quite receptive, but the critics certainly weren't: 'Casually vulgar, very brash, and very broad,' said the *New York Times*, which also accused Bruce of having 'an enormous ego'. The *New York Daily News* was even more cutting. It ran a headline, 'The Briton Not Fittin'', and went on to say, 'Forsyth does everything except wear a lampshade. He'd be a riot at a neighbour's wedding, but not on Broadway.' Some were more brutal still, calling him 'Uriah Heep on Speed' and 'absolutely average'. The only decent review came from the *New York Post*: 'The man amuses and charms,' it announced.

Of course, part of the problem was that Bruce's humour simply wasn't of the kind to go down well across the pond. The British audience treated his insults as they were intended: as light-hearted banter. The Americans took it all too literally. And Bruce's background, learning his trade as he toured around the provinces, did not prepare him for the very different atmosphere of Broadway. It might have made him a natural for television shows featuring extended audience participation, but it was not training for where he was now.

Initially, Bruce took the criticism on his not unsubstantial chin. 'I've come here to sow seeds,' he said. 'First nighters can be difficult, but I think I've won them over. It's been my life's ambition to appear on Broadway.' Bruce never did make it on Broadway, or anywhere else in the United States for that matter. He gamely had another go a few years later, when he hosted an American game show, something else that was deemed a failure.

There was a certain degree of malice in some people's reactions to his problems. In 1980, the art critic and jazz singer George Melly published *The Media Mob*, which had the following to say about Bruce: 'There is always a Trinder-like cocky conceit in Bruce, a patronising arrogance, a belief in his own omnipotence that makes it

difficult not to be a shade pleased at his come-uppance.
On the other hand, he has a real if shallow talent, and
thinks brilliantly on his feet.'

Meanwhile, his personal life was not going according to plan, either. There had been growing tensions in
Bruce's marriage to Anthea for some time, and now, to
the undisguised glee of many, given the age difference, it
rather abruptly fell apart. It was July 1979, and they had
only been married for six years, but Anthea's desire for
domesticity was increasingly at odds with Bruce's wish to
leap on the nearest plane and take off all over the world.
As with his first marriage, something was bound to give,
and it did.

The crunch, when it finally came, was not about work
at all. Bruce wanted to go to the West Indies to play golf,
his great passion, and asked Anthea to accompany him
with the children. She refused. 'I felt I couldn't keep taking the two babies on and off planes to be with him,' is
what Bruce remembers she said at the time. The couple
put out a brief statement through their solicitor, Brian
Eagles. 'There has been so much speculation about their
position that they thought it proper to make a formal announcement in the hope that they can now be left alone.'
Bruce got on yet another plane and jetted off to Spain to

play golf. Anthea was seen out on the town with friends: there were whispers that she had wanted to go out and party in the evenings, while an exhausted Bruce stayed at home: in fact, the opposite was true.

The timing of the separation was particularly embarrassing for Bruce, as it came out in the very week that Penny had been reliving her own memories of her marriage to Bruce, blaming his roving eye and meanness for their break-up. She said his ego had also got out of control: 'Everything was Bruce Forsyth,' she said. 'He said his whole world now revolved around being a star.' A mischievous journalist asked her if, now that the second Mrs Forsyth had departed the scene, she and Bruce would be reconciled: 'Have him back?' an appalled Penny exclaimed. 'Jesus, Mary, and Joseph, I would kill myself first. Never again.'

In an interview nearly twenty years later, Anthea said, 'I am quite antisocial. When I was with Bruce I was never the one who wanted to go to glamorous parties and premieres. I should have been born in a different skin. Wanting an average life with a home, a husband, and children is probably at odds with the way people perceive me. Everyone wanted us to be reconciled and I think even we thought that might happen. But you need space and privacy to work out things like that and we were never given the chance to do that.'

The two always spoke well of one another, and Bruce was as nice about Anthea as she was about him. 'We just grew apart,' he said in 1987. 'It was one of those things that happens, and there's nothing you can do about it. It's awfully sad, because you can't put your finger on why it happens. We got on well together and we still do, but the love faded. However hard you try, once that goes out of a relationship, there's nothing you can do to rekindle it.'

The marriage did come to rather a messy end, with Bruce divorcing Anthea on the grounds of her adultery with Swiss businessman Freddie Hoffman, who was to become her third husband. The real story, however, was rather more complex, not least because when the divorce came through four years later, Bruce had already met Wilnelia Merced, the woman who was the real love of his life. With the couple being the subject of intense pressure, gossip, and speculation, it took quite a while for all the facts to emerge.

Anthea finally revealed what had really been happening at the time: far from committing adultery, her new relationship had not actually been consummated. 'Bruce and I have always been perfectly honest with each other,' she said. 'I knew about Winnie, but the rest of the world didn't. The press, however, knew about Freddie and, as one of us had to admit adultery, I thought it might as well be me. I hadn't committed adultery when I admitted it. That's the truth. But we needed to get divorced quickly and cleanly, and I wanted to protect the children, Bruce, and Winnie. It was an ongoing saga in the press: "Who's he with? Who's she with?" The children were very young and I didn't want it to drag on until they were old enough to know what was happening.'

The split was far more harmonious than it had been from Penny, probably because both of them had found someone new. Anthea got custody of the children, but Bruce maintained regular contact, and they all ended up on good terms. 'I didn't envisage that when he and Winnie met we would end up as such good friends,' Anthea continued. 'There has never been a problem between us. Bruce has been as close to our daughters as any father has. He has been, and always will be, there for them. But he has also taught them that whatever they get in life, they have to deserve it. He has worked very hard, starting from nothing, so he has given them a good education. They both went to university and now they have to behave like grown ups. If either of them fell flat on her face, Bruce would be the first one to help, but now they pay all their own bills and don't expect a helping hand.'

Anthea herself took a little longer than her ex-husband to find a settled domestic life. She and Freddie Hoffman had a daughter, India, but Anthea went on to divorce him on the grounds of his unreasonable behaviour after sixteen years of marriage. There was some bitterness at the time, but that, too, subsided. 'He is a gentle, reserved man who was a wonderful stepfather,' Anthea said. 'Everything is now amicable between us. He adores India and she adores him. I'm repeating the same situation I have with Bruce. Of course, there was animosity at the time, but negative thoughts breed negative situations. You can't carry that hate within you.'

She did, finally, find happiness with the retired businessman David Adams, although the two never actually got married. 'I would be a liar if I was to say I'd be happy living on my own,' she said. 'I don't want to be this toughie who says: "I don't want a man in my life". David leaves me notes and sends me flowers for no particular reason. If he's in Marbella and I'm in Britain, we phone each other ten times a day. But I don't want to marry again. I believe you should be married when you have children, which I was, but marriage is a passion killer. The fact David and

I are not married is what keeps the excitement between us.' It was a somewhat surprising statement from such a conventional woman.

As for Bruce, when he met Wilnelia in 1980, he really did, at long last, find the right woman for him. 'She's given me a real sense of peace for the first time in my life,' he said years later. 'When I first met her, I had no idea it would turn out like this. She has had more influence on me than anyone else ever, that's for certain. She is the most beautiful woman. When we go out to a restaurant, every head turns. You can hear people saying, "Oh my God, isn't she lovely". But what is so wonderful is that women also like her. When they first see her, they might say, "Ooh, I wonder who she thinks she is". But once they talk to her, they become her friend. I don't know how to put it really. She's just so nice. That's the only word to describe her.'

'I know she's beautiful and everything, but she's also the nicest person I've ever met. That's what surprised me when I met her. Okay, I was attracted to her because she was so gorgeous, just like any man would be. Then when I got to know her, I was really surprised by how nice she was. So many men must have thrown themselves at her that she could have asked for anything from anybody and got it. She could have had scores of men if she wanted. But she wasn't like that. She was above all that somehow.' It was love.

But Bruce hadn't met her just yet, and as well as resuming his bachelor lifestyle, he then did what he always did: immersed himself in work. This time it was to be a new game show, called *Play Your Cards Right*. The 'nice to see you' catchphrase made a comeback on this show, as did a new one: 'You don't get anything for a pair, not in this game.'

The show, which aired on ITV between 1980 and 1987, was based on an American game, *Card Sharks*. It was to be one of Bruce's great successes, and he was to return several times over the following decades for various revivals and one-offs. Ironically, Bruce was not a natural at the card table. 'I've always been a very unlucky gambler,' he said. 'I could go to Las Vegas and not win one bet. I learnt that in the early days when I went into show business. There was always loads of time to spare because you only worked in the evening. In the daytime you went to the movies, or the snooker hall, or sat around a fire and played a game of cards. I always lost money. Some people are always lucky and some, like me, are not.'

But he was lucky when it came to game shows, and so it proved again. In the first series, two individuals would compete, but from the second series it was always a couple. They would alternate as to who went first, and the questions would be based on surveys of one hundred people. The competitor would guess how many of the one hundred people gave a specific answer to the question, and the second would guess if the real number was higher or lower than the guess. If the first couple got the answer exactly right, they would win a case of champagne; if the second lot were right, they would get control of the cards. And so on. (There were various more complex rules, too.)

Bruce displayed his usual genius at dealing with the audience, as well with coming up with numerous phrases that have gone into light entertainment history. These included, 'Oh, you've cheered me up,' 'What do points make? Prizes!,' 'Don't touch the pack, we'll be right back,' and the slightly more lengthy, 'I'm the leader of the pack, which makes me such a lucky Jack, but oh Brucie, there's a pair of cuties, here's my darling dealing beauties.'

Bruce was back where he belonged, but he wasn't neglecting his stage work. It is often and correctly observed that a person's success depends not on how he responds to what goes well, but how he responds to failure, and even Bruce's most ardent fans would find it hard to admit that his stint on Broadway had gone down well. Nonetheless, he put it behind him – bravely, some would say – and returned to the stage in 1980 at Fairfield Halls in Croydon. He put on a virtuoso performance, utterly undiminished by what had gone before. 'Anyone here from Glasgow? Good, got your knife with you?' was one typically barbed remark. He gave it his all: singing, tap dancing, and hosting a *Generation Game* before demanding (and getting) a standing ovation: 'Come on; get up out of your seats. I deserve it,' he cried.

What was all the more remarkable was that Bruce was doing all this with a broken arm. He'd had a fall and yet the show was going on. 'It is a shame, it has disrupted the show, it means I can't play the piano, or do any of the more physical gags I wanted to,' he said afterwards. 'I'm back in Britain now until February, when my new game show begins on London Weekend. I'm very optimistic about the new show and no, I don't see this broken arm as an omen. It really doesn't bother me any more what the papers say when I know at live shows I can find an audience like this one tonight.'

It is a mark of his versatility that Bruce did well out of

the next few years. He had his game show, which was proving enormously popular, but many of his fellow comics of
the old school were beginning to fall by the way. Times
were changing and alternative comedy was becoming the
new rock 'n' roll. As early as 1978, Bruce was the subject
of a vicious attack by Peter Cook on the Derek and Clive
album *Ad Nauseam*, in a segment entitled 'Brucie'. Cook
and Moore were not alternative comedians as such, but
the crew on *Not The Nine O'Clock News*, were, however,
and they were not alone in having a go. Bruce took it re-
markably well. The following week, as Mel Smith was de-
livering an apology for the attack, adding that Mr Forsyth
was unable to deal with these unpleasant snipes personally, Bruce made a brief, silent appearance, in which he
pushed a custard pie into Mel's face.

And that is, perhaps, what saved him: his ability to
laugh at himself. Then again, of course, the wave of alternative comedians appealed mainly to the young, and the
middle-aged and older audiences had not disappeared.
It was simply that they were not being catered to in the
way they once had been – a trend that, inexplicably, has
never been reversed to this day. In the frenetic search
for young viewers, television seems to have forgotten
that the actual majority of viewers – and those with the

spending power – are older. It was this crowd that adored Bruce and continued to support him.

Bruce's television work continued outside of the game shows. He continued to act, appearing in *Anna Pavlova*, *Magnum PI*, and, in what could have been a different sort of career breakthrough but wasn't, *Slinger's Day*. This was a programme that actually started out as *Tripper's Day*, with Leonard Rossiter in the title role, but after his untimely death in 1984, the show was revamped and, two years later, appeared with Bruce in the lead. He played a dour supermarket manager called Cecil Slinger, but the show didn't take off, and only ran for eleven episodes.

Could Bruce have been a television sitcom star? It's hard to tell. He has undoubted qualities as an actor, but what the public wanted was not Bruce playing a role: it was Bruce as himself. He went on to voice many regrets about not pushing forward his career as a song-and-dance man, but there weren't many other British entertainers of his era who were as good at doing what Bruce did. Game shows might not be the equivalent of television caviar, but it requires enormous skill to run them properly, and if he hadn't had that skill, Bruce would have been forgotten long ago.

Now in his mid-50s, he was about to embark on an entirely new stage in his life. There was still very considerable career success to come – along with a few rough spots – but, for all his drive, ambition, and energy Bruce was finally going to tone it down a gear. During his marriage to Anthea Redfern he had spoken about relaxing more than he used to, but it was hard to escape the impression that work still ruled the roost for him: everything else came second.

All that was about to change. Not only did Bruce have nothing more to prove, but also he had, at long last, met the woman who really was right for him. She was another beauty queen – indeed, that's how they met – but it was not just her stunning and exotic appearance that entranced Bruce: it was a genuine sweetness of temperament, together with that unmistakeable chemistry that binds some couples together. Bruce had found his soul mate, at last.

When Bruce Met
Wilnelia

IT WAS 1983, and a whole new Bruce Forsyth was beginning to emerge. In January that year, he'd married his long-term girlfriend Wilnelia Merced in New York, both the time and the place arranged for the convenience of her family, who were coming over from Puerto Rico. The honeymoon had lasted eight weeks, flitting between Hawaii, New Zealand, Hong Kong, Italy, and Spain, where they'd just bought a home. And then, on returning to England, months had been devoted to redecorating the house in Wentworth, too. It was in stark contrast to Bruce's first honeymoon, which was, in effect, a working holiday, followed up by a frenetic search for more jobs once back in Britain. Bruce Forsyth, Mr Energy Incarnate, was finally beginning to calm down.

Bruce was aware of the change in himself, too. 'I've made a lot of people laugh saying I've been semi-retired this year, and if you'd ever asked me, I would have said I'd get bored not working,' he said. 'But I don't. Should

the day ever come when I retire from show business, I
know I can take it.'

Utterly absorbed with his new young wife and making
a home with her, Bruce had scarcely noticed the passing
of the months. 'I didn't realise how time consuming it
is having decorators in,' he said. 'I don't think any of us
realises just how we'd react, in any walk of life, by taking a few months off. How much good it does you. I'd
always enjoyed having some free time, but never put it
to the test and always imagined it would be boring to do
nothing. That I could be so happy not working has come
as a surprise. I don't have to work all the months God
gives me, it just means I give the income tax inspector a
little less. I won't do panto anymore, or summer season.
I don't have to knock myself out in that way. So long as I
do my television and a few one-nighters, the rest of the
time I can sit back. And, of course, be much more keen
when something comes along that I want to do. In fact,
I'm working on a new show for Thames, which should
be fun.'

All off this boiled down to one person alone: Wilnelia.
When they met, she was twenty-three and Bruce nearly
thirty years her senior: for him, clearly, it was love at
first sight. 'She is the most beautiful woman,' he said,

fourteen years into the marriage and still sounding like a besotted teenager. Wilnelia quite clearly felt the same way about Bruce. She could, indeed, have had her pick of men and the fact that she chose a British comic thirty years her senior said a good deal about their relationship. 'I have to say it has to be chemistry,' she said. 'It was something I never felt before but I knew I was in love when I married him. That is the only explanation.' And he made her laugh. 'When he asked me [to marry him], I knew what I wanted to do' she said. 'I didn't care if it only lasted five years. I knew it would be the happiest five years of my life.'

She was to cause a sea change in Bruce's attitude to life right from the start. He didn't just want to be married to her; he wanted to be with her, all the time. His previous wives must have viewed it all with disbelief. 'I've always made time for us,' he said in an interview just before his eightieth birthday. 'I've never worked more than six months in the year. More recently, I've never worked more than three or four months. That sort of life suits me very well.'

Bruce first caught sight of Wilnelia in the middle of his marriage to Anthea, in 1975. He was watching Miss World on television and saw her win the title, the youngest Miss World ever, at the age of seventeen. 'I just flicked on the television at the end, saw her and thought, isn't she gorgeous, and that was it,' he recalled. It was to be some years yet before they finally met.

Bruce certainly had no clue about what was to happen to him in his personal life. He had two failed marriages behind him, and five children, so why go out searching for a third wife? 'I'd got to the stage when I'd thought I would never fall in love again,' he said. 'I'd been through it all, marriage and divorce, the lot. The last thing I was thinking of the night I met Wilnelia was falling in love. I'd reached the point where I was doubtful I ever wanted to get involved again. My life had taken a certain road, it didn't involve a serious relationship and that was it. I was quite happy living on my own, I'd done it before, and I didn't get lonely, so it didn't worry me. But when I met Wilnelia, I couldn't believe that anyone could be so nice and so unspoilt after being through what she had as Miss World. She had a very rare quality.'

When they did actually meet face to face it was, needless to say, at a beauty contest. 'Meeting Wilnelia was luck,' Bruce recalled. 'It was November 1980. I'd been asked to judge Miss World at the Royal Albert Hall and had accepted. Then, when I found they wanted me for two whole days, I said there was no way I could fit it in. I'd dismissed it; at the last minute they came back and asked me for the one day and I accepted. Getting there changed so many things. There's no way I would have been sailing past Puerto Rico, seeing my darling Wilnelia, an island girl in a sarong, saying, "Hello, Englishman". So meeting her was such luck.'

'She's sweet and gentle – she says I'm more fiery and Latin than she is. One of the things that attracted me to her that night, apart from her beauty and her lovely long hair, is that she has a very unspoilt nature. All through her working life, even when she was in New York, she's always gone back home to her parents. It's a very close family.'

Of course, even for a man as experienced at meeting beauty queens as Bruce, there were a few early glitches, starting with Wilnelia's unusual name. As she was announced as Miss World, Bruce couldn't quite make it out. 'I couldn't work out what was said,' he recalled. 'When she told me her nickname was Winnie, I said, "You can't have that as a name. In England, it's a name for old ladies".' Unmoved, Winnie remains Winnie to this day.

But there were still obstacles to be overcome. Wilnelia was not alone that night. 'I can remember interviewing some of the contestants at the Albert Hall when she came in,' said Bruce. 'I thought, "Isn't she lovely," but she had a man with her whom I assumed was her boyfriend, so I thought she wasn't available. All the time we were in there, I could feel she was looking at me, and I kept glancing back in between asking Miss Turkey what she ate for Christmas dinner – it turned out to be turkey. Wilnelia was such a lovely-looking girl. Then, when all the judges were introduced, I tried to remember her name – which was awfully difficult – but at least I knew she was a former Miss World. Eric Morley was sitting between us and every time he got up, we had a quick chat. I wasn't flirting. I didn't even have any thoughts about that, what with her boyfriend; it was just a bit of fun to pass the evening. But I kept wishing that Eric would stand up more often.'

As he relates it, Bruce, by then a man in his mid-50s, sounded more like a jittery teenager with a crush on the prettiest girl in the class than one of the giants of British entertainment. And just like a teenager, he was unsure what to do next. After the contest was over, everyone repaired to a ball at London's Hilton Hotel, where Bruce and Wilnelia were allocated seats at one of the two tables for the judges. But Wilnelia had disappeared, and Bruce wasn't sure where to sit down. 'I was just like a school kid, in a state of high anxiety,' he said.

Finally, Wilnelia returned and sat down. Bruce immediately grabbed the chair opposite her. 'That way I could look straight at her, even though it was difficult to talk, but at least I could still smile,' he said. 'Then suddenly the table was empty, except for the two of us, and I asked her where her boyfriend had gone. She said, "Oh, he's not my boyfriend, just a good friend". I couldn't believe it, it was like a lifetime of Christmases all coming at once. So I asked her to dance, and then for the next few minutes kept saying, "Are you sure he's not your boyfriend?" because I didn't fancy some karate chop.' Nonetheless, the evening just got better and better. 'And even between the dances, we kept dancing,' was Bruce's enigmatic description of the events.

At the end of the evening, Bruce found Wilnelia a cab and asked her to ring him the next day at the Palladium. This was not what Wilnelia – who grew up in the rather more conventional Caribbean, where the men did the ringing and not the women – was used to. But it had to be up to her, because she was in the middle of moving and didn't have her new number. And so, finally, she made that call.

'There was something about Bruce that impressed me and made me think he was special,' she recalled. 'I'd met so many men since I'd been Miss World, and they all just wanted to be seen with a pretty girl and say they'd been out with me. But Bruce wasn't like them. He'd made sure he was sitting at the right table, but he didn't rush anything – he waited for the right moment. I was wondering if the evening would be over before he even asked me for a dance. Then, when he held me in his arms, it just felt right. When he said goodnight, he didn't even try to kiss me on the cheek, he just gently kissed my hand. Men expect so much on the first night – because they've bought you dinner, they think they can have everything. But Bruce wasn't like that; he was a gentleman. He had the sort of values you just don't find in younger men. I sensed he was someone special and even though I wasn't looking for a relationship, I knew I wanted to see him again.'

In an unusual reversal of roles, meanwhile, Bruce was on tenterhooks at the Palladium, waiting for Wilnelia to ring. 'I told the doorman I'd be in my dressing room between rehearsals, and I stayed in there as long as I could,' he recalled. 'I was on tenterhooks with excitement – I knew I'd met someone really special.'

Wilnelia clearly thought so too, but she didn't have the faintest idea who her new admirer was. This might have been part of the appeal, for Bruce. For just as Wilnelia had often been a target for men who were only interested in being seen with her, rather than her as a person, so Bruce would often have been of interest to women who were interested in his fame, wealth, and status, rather than his personality. Wilnelia couldn't be interested in any of that, as she'd never heard of him previously, and couldn't quite understand the reaction he provoked: cars hooting, people waving and shouting and the like.

'I just thought Bruce had a lot of friends,' she explained. 'And when he said he was going to do a show at The Talk of the Town, I thought he might be a warm-up man before the main entertainment. It never occurred to me he was well known or someone special because he didn't behave that way.' Bruce recalled it with some degree of amusement. 'It wasn't until she came to see me at The Talk of the Town that she actually saw what I do on stage,' he said. 'I took some tapes of my specials for her to see and it was a bit like doing an audition.'

The courtship was now going strong, although neither immediately realised it would end in matrimony – Bruce was still technically married to Anthea, at the time. But

it wasn't long before the subject came up. To begin with
the pair of them were flying all over the world to meet up
– Wilnelia was still a model and appeared in a television
soap in Venezuela – until finally they managed to spend
a whole summer together and were so miserable at the
thought of being apart, the decision was all but made for
them. 'We knew it was going to come to an end and she'd
have to leave,' said Bruce. 'After she'd gone, the house
seemed terribly empty. But before she left, I'd said that
we should think about getting married. It was something
I wanted, but I wanted Wilnelia to think about it, too, and
see how she felt.'

There were other problems to overcome, too, and the
most obvious was the age difference. Bruce had come
in for a huge amount of stick when he married Anthea
Redfern; now he was proposing to set up home with a
still younger woman. There were her parents to think
about, and his daughters, who were now nearing their
thirties. What would everyone say? 'It could have been
the trickiest of situations, the girls meeting a stepmother
who is the same age,' said Bruce. 'If they hadn't got on,
it would have been so destructive, however much we'd
loved one another. In the end, it could have cost everything – my love and my daughters. As it is, they love her,

which is wonderful, and they all get on marvellously. It gives me such happiness.' Wilnelia recalled how nervous she was, too. 'I was so worried about meeting them, that I spent about five hours changing clothes, because I wanted to look older than I was, which was so silly,' she said. 'In the end I just decided to be myself. I'm young and that's it. We ended up having a marvellous time and they've given me so much good advice, it's like having lots of sisters.'

Of course, it would have helped that Bruce's three oldest daughters were used to seeing their father with women other than their mother, and so would have had no problem with that aspect of the situation. Indeed, they were probably just delighted that he had found someone to give him happiness and stability again. But with Wilnelia's parents, it was a different matter. She took years to tell them about the relationship, not least because her father was two years younger than her fiancé.

'I didn't tell my parents for a long time, because I wanted to be sure that this was the right relationship,' she recalled. 'There seemed no point in upsetting them. Maybe they expected me to marry someone like Prince Charles! In the end, I said, "Mummy, I've found the man of my dreams, the man I want to spend the rest of my life with, I'm in love with him, and he's really special". I then told her about all his good points, how kind and caring he is, the fact that he doesn't smoke or drink very much, likes dancing and all the things I enjoy, that he's very athletic and amusing, and how much he loves me. Then I said, "There's just one problem". And then I told her he was older. There was a long silence, and then she said, "How old?" But she knew he was the first and only man I've ever been in love with and that's what mattered.'

'When I met Bruce, I never thought about him being fifty-five. Being with him is like being with a young man because he has so much energy. He also knows what women like, he's so thoughtful and romantic, he always leaves little notes around the house for me to find, and if he has to change something because of work, he'll always send flowers. He never forgets.'

Finally, the proposal arrived, with Bruce going down on bended knee, like the old traditionalist he clearly was. 'It seemed the right way,' he recalled. 'It was a big decision for her. I had been married twice before with grown-up children and she was working in New York at the time and going back to Puerto Rico where her family live. We were at the Turnberry Hotel in Scotland. I said to her, "Really think about this. Take your time". It was sensible, because if you try to rush a lady into that kind of situation, it could be trouble, especially as she was only twenty-three at the time.'

Wilnelia did not accept straight away. She did, after all, have a life of her own, and so took a while to decide whether this was the right thing for her to do. 'She returned to New York and we spoke on the phone all the time,' said Bruce. 'I went to see her a couple of times there and also in Puerto Rico. A couple of months later, after she'd thought it out, she said yes. I used to phone her in New York about eleven o'clock our time, but five hours earlier there, and say, "Doing anything tonight?" And she'd say, "I'm going out to dinner with some people and we might go to a night club". And I'd say, "Have a lovely time, enjoy yourself", and then I'd go and put the phone down and go quietly crazy.'

'Who was she with? But I'd never say, "Please don't go out", although I was on my own in London. Later, Winnie told me how much she appreciated the cool way I played it. There's nothing worse than trying to completely possess a woman. She says now that if I had, she would have thought, "Who wants to be married to a man like that who won't let me go out with friends?" Some men check up on their wives all the time, phoning the beauty salon or wherever, but what is life all about if there isn't trust or understanding?'

Once the two were married, Wilnelia adapted well to her new home. 'She'd always loved England,' Bruce said. 'It was a very lucky place for her, and her ambition had been to come here. She is learning to play tennis and I'm teaching her to play golf. Being tall, she's the making of a good golfer. She paints and sculpts and likes to do a little modelling work, too.'

In other words, she was pretty much Bruce's ideal. By far the most stylish of Bruce's three wives, Wilnelia enjoyed exactly the same things he enjoyed. She'd been a celebrity in her own right before she met him, and so she understood something about the pressures and problems caused by fame. Bruce's pride in her was immense and at the same time, he seemed more prepared to take her needs into consideration than he had done with his earlier marriages. Right from the start, the two spent lengthy periods in her native Puerto Rico, which meant Wilnelia was never separated from her own, close-knit family.

Back in those early days, there was also the question of whether the two would have children of their own. 'That is something we've yet to discuss and plan,' said Bruce. 'Right now we agree we're happy as we are.' Of course, his children with Anthea were still young: in 1983, the year he and Wilnelia got married, Charlotte was seven and Louisa six. And just as Bruce paid an increasing amount of attention to his wives as time went by, so exactly the same applied to his children. His first three daughters didn't see a great deal of their father as they were growing up, as he was out to make his name. With Charlotte and Louisa, who lived nearby, it was different.

'They adore Winnie,' said Bruce. 'They're lovely kids and we all play together and have lovely weekends. I'm a different father than I was to my elder group (I'm a grandfather twice, you know). When my first three daughters were children, I was so much busier, so I didn't get to see much of them. Yet I'm very close to them now, much closer than I ever thought I'd be. I think it's because they know more about me and, whichever way their lives have gone, I've always been there to help or advise, but give them a free rein, too.'

Nineteen eighty-three was also the year that he had a part in *Anna Pavlova*, in which he played Sir Alfred Butt, the man responsible for introducing the great Russian ballerina to the English stage. It was a Russian film, and Bruce seemed a little bemused and yet delighted at the way it had gone. 'I made them laugh,' he said. 'I might be able to do a double act with Ken Livingstone and have Arthur Scargill as our agent. All comics are actors. I think actors would find it difficult to do our job, but most comics are capable of doing acting parts.'

With his relationship with Wilnelia going so well, Bruce was able to let the past rest in the past. And there was further joy when, a few years into the marriage, Wilnelia gave birth to Jonathan Joseph Enrique Forsyth, known as JJ, on 10 November 1986, Bruce's sixth child and first son. Although he was thrilled on his own account, it was also an example of Bruce making sure Wilnelia was happy, especially given the age difference and the fact that Bruce was already a father.

'I think a man should go along with a woman's wishes, particularly when there's an age difference,' he said. 'I've seen women with older husbands who say they've made an agreement not to have children and I've seen the sadness in their eyes. For many women, part of their life is being a mother. It's very sad not to fulfil that. If Wilnelia hadn't wanted children, that would have been fine, too. We were perfectly happy. I didn't mind whether I was a dad or not, but she's such a wonderful mother and I knew she would be. In the end, all I wanted was for her to be happy.'

Bruce has always maintained that he'd been so delighted that he had healthy children that their gender was irrelevant, but even so, he was clearly thrilled to have a boy. Indeed, he doted on the little chap. 'I went into the bathroom the other day,' said Wilnelia, in an interview a few months after JJ was born. 'We have a very large bath, and Bruce and JJ were in it together – Bruce playing with boats while JJ was just lying there. Just before Christmas, he said that he wanted to buy a train set for his son, and I said he's far too young. Then I realised Bruce wanted one so he could play with it himself. Although he always said he didn't mind what we had as long as the baby was happy and healthy, I know he was thrilled to have a son. They watch American football together on television and I walked in once to hear Bruce chatting. He just looked round and said, "Not now, dear, this is men's talk". I haven't just got one boy, you see, I've got two – JJ and Bruce.'

Bruce himself accepted that it was his new, changed attitude that was making the marriage such a success. 'About ten years ago, I realised that my life seemed like all work, I always seemed to be signed up for about eighteen months in advance, so I took some time off,' he said in an interview in 1987. 'I thought that I'd get bored, but

I didn't. I really enjoyed it. There seemed to be so many other things to do. If I'd met Wilnelia before then, it probably would not have worked because I would have been too busy. As it is, I'm home much more of the time with her and our little boy JJ. I take time off when I want, I now know how to say, "no". I don't need work to turn me on; I don't need my name in lights to make me feel good. I still enjoy working, but it's not everything – my wife and the little fellow are more important. With my daughters, who are all grown up now, I was only half a dad because I was away so much. I've been terribly lucky that we've all become so much closer as we've got older.'

By this time the couple had bought an apartment in Puerto Rico and were spending at least four months of the year out there. And in Puerto Rico, it was Wilnelia who was the star, not Bruce, something he would probably have found intolerable in his earlier marriages, but was positively gleeful about now. And it had its advantages. 'No one knows him there, so he can lead a normal life, go shopping in supermarkets, and wander around,' said Wilnelia. 'Over there they call him Mr World, because he's my husband and I'm more famous than him.'

The birth of JJ did bring home the fact that there was an age difference and the couple acknowledged that.

'I know that I'm married to an older man, and there's no point in worrying about that,' said Wilnelia in 1987, twenty-one years before Bruce's eightieth birthday. 'If I have ten years of happiness with Bruce, that's a lot more than most people have in their entire lives. All I know is that he's the only man in the world I want to be with.'

Mortality was, however, on Bruce's mind. The comedians Eric Morecambe and Leonard Rossiter both died years before their time in the early 1980s, and Bruce had known them both. It made him more determined than ever to have a life outside of work. 'The death of people such as Eric Morecambe and Leonard Rossiter made me realise that I'd made the right decision to be more relaxed and enjoy life,' he said. 'I don't want people standing at my memorial service saying he was a great trouper, so sad he was only fifty-nine.' It was a good call on his part.

Par For The Course

AS HE NEARED his sixties, Bruce was adopting an altogether more relaxed attitude towards his career. One passion, though, was as strong as ever: golf. Bruce's passion for golf extended back to when he was nineteen years old and staying in digs in Dundee. One morning he was forced out of bed at 7am, dragged to Carnoustie golf course, and introduced to a sport that was to captivate him for the rest of his life. His love of golf, along with the fact that he's a trained dancer, may well have a great deal to do that he is still so healthy at eighty: outdoors exercise has always been a part of his life. In 1989, such was his love of the game that he published a book about it, *Golf ... is it only a game?* To him, it was far more than that. He described himself as a 'pretty adequate ten-handicap player,' and, in the fourteen years of BBC2's Celebrity Pro-Am, he's played in every one.

By this time in his life, he'd played with almost anyone who was anyone on the course: Seve Ballesteros, Ian

Woosnam, Nick Faldo, and Sam Torrance, to name but a few. He loved them all. 'It's difficult to think of a pro I have played with who hasn't been a one hundred per cent gentleman,' he said. 'But they are different in Pro-Am games to what they are in tournaments. Seve laughs and jokes, he's the most wonderful guy. Of course, in an actual tournament he doesn't talk much. When he played Arnold Palmer, they both had a completely different look in their eyes. They were men with a different attitude.'

And he knew everything about them, too. 'Everyone wonders how a guy as tiny as Ian Woosnam hits the ball as far, if not further, than a lot of the long hitters,' he said. 'One of the things about him is that he has strong forearms. That's why there is a picture in the book of me arm wrestling with him. I reckon it can't be the forearms, because I was dead level with him.'

Such is his passion for the game that he possesses a much-treasured letter. It reads, 'We the undersigned, being of sound mind and body, do solemnly swear and declare that Bruce Forsyth is in our opinion the most proficient celebrity at the game of golf we have so far en-countered.' Lee Trevino and Seve Ballesteros signed it. 'I was playing golf and they said how good I was, so I asked them to put it in writing,' Bruce blushingly explained.

Golf was, however, one of the few things he did not entirely share with Wilnelia, although she was learning to play the game. 'I am so busy doing other things such as painting and sculpting and tennis,' she said. 'I do not have patience. I do not have a handicap yet, but I will one day,' she said. Bruce himself was in no doubt that his wife would soon be a whiz on the course. 'Winnie has the most wonderful swing; she has a natural talent,' he said. And, of course, little JJ was learning to play as well: 'He's been swinging a little plastic club since he was thirteen months, just after he learned how to walk,' said Bruce. 'He's got a great little swing. He's going to be tremendous.'

For some years now, Bruce had been emphasising the difference between on-stage Brucie and off-stage Bruce, and by this time the two quite different characters were clear in his mind. 'Winnie knows me as Bruce, the man she married – not Brucie,' he explained. 'It doesn't mean that I don't go into him from time to time at home; it can diffuse a strain. If something is going wrong, I can joke about it.'

Rather interestingly, Bruce credits understanding this dual persona with a stunt pulled in 1967. Someone took a photograph of him, cut it in half, and then made two different pictures, one using the features on the right side of his face and the other using the features on the left. Two entirely different portraits emerged. 'The result was quite amazing,' said Bruce. 'In one picture – because of a little bubble on the side of my nose – I look like the village idiot. In the other, like some dynamic tycoon, a fantastic businessman.'

'I then realised the truth of what my old friend Alfred Marks once told me. "Your secret," he said, "is that you let the audience behind the façade of Big Brucie up there on stage." And he was right. I can be quite shy, although some people might not believe it. The shy Bruce is in the wings waiting to go on and asking himself, "Will they like me?" The other one, big Brucie, says, "Of course they will. Or you'll give them their money back". I don't care. Bruce is certainly not a stand-up comic. I couldn't tell you a joke now if you asked. I don't have to be centre stage – that's because I'm a jack-of-all-trades, and a master of none. So the Bruce waiting for his queue is completely different from Brucie who, when the music starts, walks into my body and takes over. But I couldn't keep up with that TV Brucie. He'd drive me dotty. I wouldn't be able to live with him and neither would Wilnelia.'

In his mid-fifties, Bruce adopted a much more stringent diet and exercise regime than he ever had done before. He was, after all, now well into middle age, and if he wanted to keep trim and performing, which he clearly did, then he had to make sure he stayed fit. He had never been a big drinker or a smoker, and now took an even stricter approach to his health. He followed a fitness regime called Fountain of Youth, which had been created by Tibetan monks, took two royal jelly tablets before breakfast, and two garlic tablets and Efamol marine with every meal. 'I do the Tibetan workout every day. It really wakes you up and makes you feel good,' he explained.

He kept a very strict eye on what he ate, too, eating fruit all morning and a plate of raw vegetables for lunch. 'It boosts my energy levels and as a result I feel a lot healthier,' he told one interviewer. 'I am buzzing with energy and rarely catch colds. But I sometimes pig out on naughty things like doughnuts and chocolate.'

Preparing for one of his one-man shows, he also explained how he kept himself in readiness for it all. 'Yes, I have a bit of back trouble, but I do stretching exercises and I'm careful,' he said. 'With the piano playing, I can go back to it after months away, warm up the fingers, and I get all keen again. I love fiddling around with chords. As for the voice, well, I'm sensible and I don't smoke now. No cigarettes, just a puff of a cigar about twice a year.'

His new, laid back career continued apace, too. In the early 1990s, there was much excitement when he returned to the scene of one of his former glories: *The Generation Game* was brought back, with Bruce fronting it once more. He was in his element, back tormenting his audiences, and yet establishing with them a camaraderie that younger hosts couldn't hope to pull off. His hostess now was Rosemarie Ford and, again unusually, Bruce acted as his own warm-up man, which got the audience right where he wanted them before he even started recording the show.

Indeed, he enjoyed it so much that he sometimes seemed reluctant to get to the actual recording. 'It's nice to be back at the BBC,' was one typical riposte. 'I spent ten years at LWT. You know what that stands for? Limp-Wristed Television. Mind you, they bent over backwards for me.'

'We're ready now,' called the floor manager.

'Well, I'm not,' said Bruce, and went back to bantering with the audience. 'How many of you have seen me on television, but never before in the flesh? And how many of you are regretting it already?' The audience lapped it up.

One slight difference from the original show was that Bruce was much ruder to the audience this time round.

'What a coach trip you are,' he told one lot. 'You can even smell the crisps.' Nor was he sparing in his treatment of the contestants. Where once there was sympathy, now there was exasperation. He had actually done this before, way back at the London Palladium: 'Oh yes, Daisy, the onion-buncher, but you know I already know my onions,' was how he introduced one contestant in 1960. 'Not now, wait!' as Daisy started the game a little too quickly. 'For goodness sake, I've got enough problems tonight.' He turned to another contestant. 'You've really mucked it up,' he chided. What worked then still worked now.

Bruce himself put it down to his long apprenticeship so many years previously. 'I spent years enduring the frustration of being second spot comic on the variety bills – which is a killer because no one wants to know,' he said to an interviewer in 1992. 'Then came *London Palladium* and "Beat the Clock" and I was off. Now when I tell an audience where to get off, part of it is the memory of what I would have liked to tell them all those years ago, but couldn't. I can insult them now, but they don't take it seriously: for all the jokes about being in charge, they know I'm fooling myself. I can crumble and they laugh at the façade, the Forsyth Façade, because all performers should be a bit nervous.'

Philip Jones, who had been the producer of the *Bruce Forsyth Show*, also maintained that Bruce always knew when to stop. 'He's terrific at interviewing and getting the maximum fun out of people, but he steers clear of offence,' he said. 'He remembers their names. He kisses and makes up after every gag.'

Bruce himself never underestimated the importance of his relationship with the audience. It was his unique selling point. It was what set him apart in the work that he did. And that had been the case from the very beginning, when he was learning his trade. 'The audience are always my yardstick,' he said. 'I do use the camera at times, for close-up looks, as thought they are people I can confide in, but most of the time they are an infringement. To do what I do without an audience would be virtually impossible. An audience of two hundred and fifty or three hundred is all you get in a television studio, and anything under five hundred is difficult, anyway. And if you can't see them – what do you do? I'd love to do a TV show in which all these special cameras are at the back of the studio and they can just zoom in with different lenses – it would be a lovely thing of just you and the audience.'

Each show took about four days to complete, and there was a lot of hard work involved, although, as before, Bruce only met the contestants moments before the show. 'I see them as a group and tell them they can't escape now and it'll be like going to the doctor's,' he chortled. 'It's a very tricky exercise that we try to make look as easy as pie. And there are some priceless moments. One lady we had on the Christmas show hadn't understood when she was supposed to do her thing, the egg trick, blindfolded. We had to set it all up again but that time she completely messed it up and couldn't go on with the game. It was such a shame. Then, at the end, I got pairs of contestants to sing. And suddenly, there she was singing in this lovely voice – like Whitney Houston!'

Bruce refused, however, to be complacent on the back of the success of the newly re-launched show. His feet were still on the ground: he still knew how fortunate he'd been for so many years. Did he, an interviewer asked, think, 'Clever old Bruce' when the show was revived? No, he did not. 'I thought lucky old Bruce,' he said. 'How many chances do you get to do a show you first started nearly twenty years ago? I was lucky I'd left it after seven years. I thought we'd run out of ideas and I was getting stale. If I'd stayed and we'd gradually gone downhill, it would never have been revived.'

Indeed, when he looked at a few tapes of the original

show, it brought it all back. Jim Moir, the BBC's head of light entertainment, had offered the new show to Bruce over lunch: 'He said, "I know you'll want to think things through," which I did, being a Pisces,' Bruce recalled. 'Then I looked at a few old tapes. I found things I didn't remember doing, things that made me laugh, so I thought, "Why not?" And I'm so glad I did because I did have an awful lot of fun again.'

The Generation Game was another Forsyth success. When it was reintroduced on to the television screens, *The Generation Game* was put out on Friday nights, not Saturday. However, ratings started soaring upwards, from nine million to twelve million. It might not have been the twenty-plus million Bruce experienced the first time round, but it was remarkable by this point, for the simple fact there were now so many television channels around. It was finally reinstated to Saturday night, where Bruce was to continue for another five years.

He kept his hand in with other work, too. There was to be another vehicle, *Brucie's Guest Night*, in which he talked to big name Hollywood stars. 'It isn't just going to be a talk-show,' he told one interviewer. 'I'll do things with the guests – a song, a dance, or something on the piano. Talk shows have become rather stereotyped. I once stood in for Wogan for a week and, before that, there was *The Big Night* and Bette Midler was there, too. *Brucie's Guest Night* has taken me twenty years to get going, which isn't too bad. Maybe things turn out for the best. If I had done it then, instead of [the first time around], people would be saying now, "When's he going to stop it?"'

And there were to be specials, too. These were important to Bruce, for they allowed him to display the many talents he honed: singing, dancing, the shtick. 'Doing it all, the music and dancing, is more important to me than anything,' he said to one interviewer. 'I'm happy that I don't just do comedy. Comedy isn't such a dramatic thing to me. It isn't where I earn my bread and butter. I never try to dissect it the way some comedians do. I know how to get a laugh, how to time it. But if you ask me to tell a joke now, I couldn't. I don't remember a million jokes.'

Then there was the popular series *Takeover Bids* and he was also back at his beloved Palladium, too. Here he was, back to his all-singing, all-dancing, haranguing-the-audience best. How did he do it, especially baiting the audience the way he did? 'Well, every performer has an insecurity and I've always played on that,' said Bruce. 'When I was a kid and doing amateur charity shows during the war, I always drew audiences into what was going on, or going wrong. If I had an old lady on the piano who wasn't playing tempo for my tap, I'd stop, walk over, and tell her so. And tell the audience, too. You know, so I didn't get the blame.'

More and more, the stage Brucie was being differentiated from the quieter Bruce at home, and the man himself was able to switch alarmingly quickly between the two. 'At times, I burst into Brucie unexpectedly, and the sense of humour is there a lot of the time,' he said. 'But I'm so glad I've learnt the art of relaxing. In fact, only a short while before going on, I can still be feeling quite calm. But then this idiot sort of appears from nowhere, he gets inside my body, rushes me on stage – and I become "him" – but I'm certainly not always him. I have these peculiar expressions that I go into. But I don't sit at the mirror practising faces or anything. I know I have certain looks for certain moments, which seem to have worked for me over the years. Now I don't know if I've got any new expressions, but the old ones come in rather handy.'

Bruce was now also a very wealthy man. He had never lived beyond his means, liked to boast that he'd always paid the tax bill on time, and was now living in some considerable style. There was the mansion in Virginia

Water, Surrey, on the edge of Wentworth golf course, and his trademark Bentley, with the licence plate BFE – Bruce Forsyth Entertainer. He took great pleasure in his mansion and the surrounding gardens, as well. 'I love pretty countryside and grounds laid out beautifully,' he said. 'My mother was the same. She loved her garden, even though it was only a narrow strip. She'd have loved it here. Sometimes, I imagine I see her here.' The house was also done out in a very striking style: a bright blue carpet in the hall led up to the drawing room, which was covered in a black carpet, on which there was a glass coffee table held aloft by four griffins. Huge vases were dotted about, one lamp was in the shape of a spitting cobra, and a massive ormolu clock adorned the mantelpiece.

Given his circumstances – wealth, marriage to a Miss World, status, the works – Bruce was asked if he was still able to see himself on the same level as the people who came to see him. 'Yes, because I see myself as a member of a team,' he said. 'I relate to other members of the team, and I relate to the audience. I know they have their ups and downs. I drive through the same traffic jams as them.' And he genuinely empathised with the audience. 'I love it when people win, and I hate it when people lose,' he said.

The Generation Game in its new incarnation, meanwhile, was a great success. While not garnering quite the ratings it once had, it proved to be another success, although Bruce did leave on a slightly sour note, one of several that were to strike in the late 1990s.

'I am very happy to have left the BBC,' he said in 1995. 'They don't really cater for family audiences any more. It is very obvious they have their particular favourites and perhaps I'm not one of them. I have nothing in common with them, and I'm glad they have nothing in common with me. Although I have run out of ambitions these days, one of them was definitely to get out of the BBC.' That was, of course, by no means the end of the story. But at that point, he'd had enough.

As the years went by, the doubters – and there had been a fair few – about his marriage to Wilnelia were ever more clearly being proved wrong. The marriage was not only a happy and stable one, but also Wilnelia actually managed to bring in the girls from Bruce's previous two relationships to form a family unit. Bruce was well aware of how lucky he was. 'Once you've been there twice and it hasn't worked, you do begin to think, "Can it ever work?"' he mused. 'And the first time I met Winnie, I didn't want to get serious about anyone. If anything, I was dead against it. But she just had this wonderful love-liness. Yes, she was beautiful, but she was also so nice.' Nice is a word Bruce uses frequently to describe Winnie: it is clearly the quality that has made the marriage work so well.

She was very good at keeping all the wider elements of the family together. 'My favourite day of the year is Father's Day, when my five daughters come over to visit me,' he said when he was in his mid-sixties. 'I love it because I can sit around all day being waited on by my lovely girls and they spoil me rotten. It's much better than Christmas, because it's *my* day. It is probably unusual to have three different families that are so united. But there are no funny feelings between us. My daughters all love my wife. They come over to see her as much as they do me, and the love they bring into this house in unbelievable. You can feel it all around you.'

And while Bruce was certainly not a new man, he was finding real joy in having a young son with whom he could spend much more time than he did with his daughters when they were young. 'I'm not very good with young children, and I'm certainly no good at changing nappies,' he confessed. 'But I love the age that JJ is now [eight]. I can take him onto the golf course or to a Spurs football match and we love watching sport together on television. He is at the stage now where I can reason and have conversations with him. I love my daughters, but it is wonderful to have a boy. Boys are certainly much noisier and more excitable than girls, which was hard for me while I was doing *The Generation Game* for the past five years. When you are tired after working all day and he is kicking up a storm, it can be difficult. But since finishing *The Generation Game*, I am already much more relaxed with him. It's very important for me to be a proper dad.'

'I would love to be twenty years younger so that I can enjoy seeing what happens to him and to my younger daughters in later years,' said Bruce rather wistfully. 'It saddens me that I might not be able to help JJ at a time when he might need me a lot. But if I can give him a good start in life, which so many children don't have, and if he knows he comes from a loving couple, then that can influence him for the rest of his life. I was very lucky to have a loving mother and father who did everything they could to get me into this business. Without their help and encouragement I wouldn't have made it.'

'I just want him to know how much love we have for him. Because he has been born into an affluent background, I do try not to spoil him, but it is hard. We went to stay at the Dorchester Hotel the other day, and he couldn't wait to get into the room and ring for room service. I had to make it clear to him that it was a very special day and he would have to be a very good boy if he wanted to come again. I have to be strict, but he does take it all in very good heart.'

Bruce still had plenty of other work going on, including *Bruce's Price is Right*, followed by *Play Your Cards Right*. But it did seem that retirement was increasingly on his mind. By the age of sixty-eight, he was clearly wondering if he should call it a day: 'It depends on what happens, but my plan is to give it another two or three years and then I'll make a clean break,' he said. 'I won't return in guest spots. It's sad when performers make comebacks. I hated to see Fred Astaire, who I idolised all my life, doing "bit" parts and looking so old and past it. I wanted to remember him as he was. I love being on stage and enjoy the applause and laughter, but fortunately I'm not one of those who need it to make life worthwhile.'

His work schedule was now just what he wanted. Bruce was rumoured to be on a contract of about £1 million for *Play Your Cards Right*, while *Bruce's Price is Right* had a filming schedule that suited him perfectly: seventeen programmes in just over a week and a half. 'I always like it when they say, "He's one of the top earners,"' said Bruce to one interviewer. 'I've never had the luxury of a fixed-format show before – *The Generation Game* was much more difficult, because there are five games every time and you're always trying to find a different way of doing them.'

On both shows, his rapport with the audience was as strong as it had ever been. 'I like to make sure they're happy and know exactly what they're doing,' he said. 'I'm lucky enough to get away with being semi-rude, because the contestants accept it as a bit of fun. At the end, they'd put their head in a gas oven if I asked. You're on a knife-edge, though, and it's hit and miss. Those who look as if they're going to be good sometimes freeze. I love something to go wrong, because I can play off it. The worse thing for me is when it goes too smoothly.'

Of course, *Bruce's Price is Right* was a show that was based on people's greed: what did he think about that? 'Greed has always come into it, but the contestants are usually lovely people,' protested Bruce. 'There wasn't a greedy one in the first series of *Bruce's Price is Right*. Some miss a showcase of £25,000 and accept it graciously. You don't see anyone getting into a temper about it. I'm honestly disappointed when they lose and elated when they win. The British like to see someone win, even if it's not them. I won't say we're always good losers, but accepting defeat graciously is a national trait.'

We've Come
A Long Way

IT WAS BRUCE'S seventieth birthday, and, fittingly, he celebrated by hosting a one-man show at the London Palladium, with a special tribute recording to be shown on ITV. Rather more traumatically, the couple discovered that Wilnelia was pregnant, but it was an ectopic pregnancy, and she had to be rushed into hospital. Bruce was at Wilnelia's side throughout. 'I couldn't have got through it without him,' she said. 'Not many men would understand just what a woman goes through in that situation, but Bruce did. I will never, ever forget that experience I shared with him. He was so caring and stayed with me in the hospital for five days without leaving my side. Once I got home, I had to recuperate for a month and was desperately down, but Bruce was there the whole time, giving constant support. He was so caring, thoughtful, and understanding."

It was a blow. JJ, then eleven, was the apple of both parents' eyes, but Wilnelia had been harbouring hopes that she would one day have a daughter. It was not to be. After that, the couple decided she would not get pregnant again, something they came to accept. Bruce was also dreadfully concerned about the impact on his wife. 'I was desperately upset for Winnie,' he said. 'It was such a tragic thing to happen. It was awful seeing someone you love going though something so painful and difficult. Thank heavens I was able to give her the help and support she needed.'

In 1999, Bruce had something else to cope with. David Liddiment, ITV's head of light entertainment, took the decision to downgrade *Play Your Cards Right* – although he wouldn't specify if it had been axed – and reschedule *The Price is Right*, moving it to the less than desirable teatime slot of 5.20pm. The audience promptly dropped from eight-and-a-half million to just over three-and-a-half million and Bruce did not take well at all. He called a press conference in a suite at the Dorchester Hotel, where he declared he would not work for ITV if Liddiment were still in charge. 'He has lied to me, stripped me of my dignity, and humiliated me,' he snapped. 'Even *Who Wants to be a Millionaire* would have no chance at that time. In all the forty years I have been in the business, I have never been treated so badly.'

He certainly wasn't taking it lying down. Bruce distributed cards to the assembled journalists, with charts showing that *Bruce's Price is Right* had a more than forty per cent share of the audience in five of the previous seven months that it had been shown: of sixteen shows recorded, however, only eleven had been shown. David Liddiment had written to Bruce apologising for this and saying they 'fell through the crack': Bruce demanded a meeting, where he asked if they were trying to phase him out. 'I would much rather someone had the guts to say to me, "It's time to call it a day,"' he said.

Nor was this all. Bruce was contracted to appear in one more series of *Bruce's Price is Right*, after which, he said, he'd had enough. 'I've always said that I would retire when I no longer get enjoyment from walking on to the studio floor, or the stage, or when my ratings go,' he said. 'That hasn't happened, so I'm simply axing myself from ITV and this man. What he's done to me, I cannot forgive him for.'

David Liddiment himself expressed sorrow. 'Bruce Forsyth is probably the greatest all-round entertainer British television has ever known, and ITV is immensely proud of its long and successful relationship with him,' he said. 'It has been a delight for me to work with him over the past three years, and I am very sorry he feels the way he does.' The damage, however, had been done.

For all of Bruce's bravado, it was a severe blow. On many occasions in the past, Bruce had thought his career could be over, but this time he felt personally wounded by the course of events. 'When you feel as though you can still perform and you have what it takes to get out there and do what you've done all your life, and all of a sudden the door's shut, what do you do?' he asked. 'How do you face that? It was a terrible feeling. I'd always said to my agent, "If ever you know that the door is closing, let me know and I'll retire gracefully". But people were coming up to me in the street, saying, "We haven't seen you in such a long while. Aren't you doing any more television?" It was the public that was making me feel ignored. That made me feel bad.'

But Bruce was a trouper. He hadn't spent almost a lifetime in show business without learning to take the bad times with the good and this was not, after all, the first time he'd had a setback in his television career. So he coped. 'I've always been very resilient,' he said. 'When you're a variety performer, you go from town to town. You'd have Monday night audiences that were so bad, you'd go out there and some guy would be reading the newspaper. So rejection is part of being a variety performer. It brings out the feeling that next week will be better. Or, I'll get something the week after that. That becomes ingrained in you.'

In 2002, Bruce made the headlines for all the wrong reasons, when his house, by now worth about £4 million, was the subject of a raid by a gang of armed robbers. Bruce himself was up in Edinburgh at the time, visiting Ronnie Corbett, and watching the Open golf – something the gang was believed to have taken into account when they staged the break-in – but returned to London as soon as he heard the news. Those in the house were tied up. Wilnelia and JJ were unhurt, but the family's housekeeper was savagely beaten and taken to hospital suffering from serious facial injuries.

It had been planned carefully. Wilnelia and JJ had gone to bed at about 11.45pm, and it was about half an hour after that that their housekeeper heard a noise. There was immediate concern as to how the robbers had managed to break in: apart from the house's extensive security system, it was in what was thought to be a very safe enclave. 'It's absolutely shocking news,' said a neighbour. 'One of the best features about living here has always been the excellent security. We're such a small

After two failed marriages, Bruce finally met the love of his life, Wilnelia Merced, and married her in 1983, when he was fifty-five. Wilnelia won Miss World at the tender age of seventeen (top picture), and was, controversially, thirty-two years younger than her husband when they married. However, theirs has been a successful union, cemented with the birth of their first and only child, and Bruce's only son, JJ (right).

Bruce poses (above) with two of his 'dealing beauties' (Victoria Brattle, left, and Sophie Allistone, right) on another of his success stories, *Play Your Cards Right*, c. 1994.

Bruce on stage with his contemporary and close friend, Ronnie Corbett, c. 1990s.

Bruce in his element with his *Price is Right* (1996), and hosting the later edition of 'Beat the Clock' (2002).

Bruce at the unveiling of his bust at the London
Palladium in 2005. It was made by his son-in-law,
Dominic Grant.

Bruce's one passion in life, apart from entertaining, is golf. He has been an avid fan of the sport since he was nineteen years old. Here he is seen playing, and enjoying a joke with actor James Nesbitt, at the All*Star Cup Golf in Wales in 2006.

Bruce proudly showing off his OBE
at Buckingham Palace in 2006.

After twenty-five years of marriage, Bruce and
Wilnelia are as happy as the day they first met.

At eighty years of age, Bruce is still as active and
vigorous as a man half his age. Here he celebrates his
eightieth birthday, and a lifetime in show business, at
the Dorchester in London with, fittingly, two beauty
queens by his side: Miss Puerto Rico (left) and
Miss England (right).

community, so any strangers tend to stick out like a sore thumb.'

'The gang must have known about the security measures at Mr Forsyth's home and must have planned this raid extremely well,' said a member of the Surrey police. 'At the time of the offence, Mr Forsyth was not at home. He was in Muirfield in Scotland watching the Open golf championship. A knife was seen in the incident and force was used.' Bruce himself was too shocked to do anything other than issue an official statement, but Ronnie Corbett was able to say a few words. 'They just knocked on the door and broke the news,' he said. 'Bruce immediately rang home, and the officers took him to the airport to catch the first flight down south. Bruce was very upset. The police told Bruce it wasn't a pleasant attack. There was a bit of agro and violence. Bruce was just relieved his family was all right. I really felt for my friend, but we are just so relieved Bruce's family are all fine.'

The family was shaken severely, and Bruce remained so for some time afterwards. 'Why wasn't I here?' he asked one interviewer two years after the event. 'It was the one night I'd been away for the whole of the year. It's not as if I go travelling up and down the country all the time. Why wasn't I here? Could I have done something to prevent it? Maybe when they'd seen me, they'd have said, "Oh, we're in Brucie's house". Maybe I could have had some sort of joke with them. Who knows what would have happened?' In reality, of course, there was a very good chance the thieves knew exactly where they were: the house was almost certainly deliberately targeted.

In the aftermath of the break-in – his housekeeper recovered fully – Bruce bought a guard dog, which he called Mace. 'It's funny to see this little Filipina give him his orders,' he said. 'She says to me, "Sah, sah, Mace, he still jump up, but he no jump on me". I say, "He's got nowhere to jump!" She's four foot ten. Lovely.'

The following year, in a clear sign that the unhappiness of the past really had been forgotten, Bruce was spotted visiting his first wife, Penny, in Brinsworth House, a show business nursing home run by the Entertainment Artistes Benevolent Fund in Twickenham. Penny was a full time resident. 'They were having tea together and could have been mistaken for a united family again,' said a fellow visitor. 'Bruce was extremely affectionate towards Penny, and seemed very concerned for her. Penny looks much younger than her age, but now has to walk with the help of a frame. Relations between Bruce and Penny began to improve when Bruce married Wilnelia, but you could see Penny was touched Bruce came to visit her in the nursing home.' It was a happier end than many would have envisaged years earlier: Penny had finally managed to put the past behind her. She had, after all, been married to Bruce for twenty years herself, and now shared not only grandchildren but also great grandchildren with him. They had all come a long way.

Have I Got A Veteran
Entertainer For You

IN THE EARLY years of the twenty-first century it seemed, as it had done on several occasions previously, that Bruce's career was coming to an end. It had been a spectacular run: now in his mid-seventies, Bruce had been part of the British entertainment industry for as long as anyone could remember. He was popular with both young and old. He was happy and settled in his private life, now spending up to six months a year in Puerto Rico with Wilnelia.

They'd had a home there for years, and Bruce revelled in the anonymity he found there, enjoying their Caribbean home, playing golf, and relaxing in the sunshine. 'It's only a tree, but it's ours,' he would say. 'It's my winter Shangri-La.' Ironically, given the fact that he had once wanted to conquer international audiences, he liked that it was Wilnelia, not him, who was the star in Puerto Rico. 'They call me Mr World,' he said.

Bruce was now absent from British television screens.

As well as his game shows, he'd also been the face of the Courts furnishing company for some years, starring in advertisements that were hugely popular. To begin with, they worked so well that they were single-handedly seen as having turned around Courts's sales, just as Twiggy was credited with having massively boosted the image of Marks & Spencer nearly a year later. In 1996, the first year he worked for them, sales leapt by thirty-three per cent. It was proof of his popularity with the public, and the company went on to use him for some years more.

Times were changing in other ways, too. In 2000, Eric Morley, the founder of the Miss World beauty pageant, died, aged eighty-two. Through his work he had had a huge impact on the lives of both Bruce and Wilnelia and both were rather shocked. 'It's a big loss to us,' said Bruce. 'I liked him tremendously, and he did so much for children around the world and a lot of people forget that. We saw a lot of him over the years, and it's a big loss to us that he has passed away.'

As far as Wilnelia was concerned, Eric and his wife, Julia, almost had become her surrogate parents after she won the title. 'He changed my life and I will always be grateful for that,' she said. 'I have so many wonderful memories of him that are precious to me. I am so disappointed he had to die this year of all years, because he was so looking forward to the fiftieth year. We had been together for many of the big events in our lives – the celebrations and birthdays. I consider him part of my family.'

Miss World had been dropped in 1988 by ITV, not least because it seemed to be out of keeping with the times – Morley had been 'very disappointed', said Wilnelia, 'because it was still a big worldwide event' – but was picked up a decade later by Channel 5. 'I think it's sad that people wanted to stop the competition,' said Bruce. 'What's wrong with someone looking good, having ambition, and winning a competition? I could never understand why he was never given an honour after all he did for charity. When you think of all the children he helped over the years, it's a big mystery.' Channel 5 was going to screen the contest's fiftieth anniversary on 30 November 2000. 'Everyone at Channel 5 is deeply shocked and saddened by the passing of Eric Morley,' said Channel 5 chief executive Dawn Airey. 'He was a legendary figure in the entertainment world and will be deeply missed.'

Bruce, on the other hand, was about to pitch himself into the lion's den and onto a show that you had to be very tough indeed to make a go of, and a show that was peopled with participants a good four decades younger – or more – than he was. It was a show that was not only utterly different from anything Bruce had done before, but also a show that had grown out of the alternative comedy movement of the early 1980s – a movement that had set itself aside from everything that Bruce and his ilk stood for. It was, of course, *Have I Got News For You*.

Ever since its long-term presenter, Angus Deayton, had been packed off a few years earlier following an episode involving cocaine and kiss-and-tell girls, *Have I Got News For You* had been entertaining a series of guest presenters with differing degrees of success. In hindsight, of course, it was showbiz genius to include Bruce in that roll call, but it may not have occurred to anyone at the time. Apart from anything else, Bruce appeared to have all but retired; on top of this, *Have I Got News For You* was not his cup of tea (it was thought) at all. Bruce was by now best known as the host of a very different type of game show, with a very different type of audience. Nor were the fearsome duo of Paul Merton and Ian Hislop to be taken on lightly. They had been the downfall of many a presenter before Bruce as, say, Piers Morgan, Edwina Currie, and Derek Hatton, to name but a few, would attest.

But that was not to be the case with Bruce. Unusually for him, it was he himself who set the ball rolling. 'I was sitting at home watching *Have I Got News For You* with my wife Winnie when she said: "You know, you could do that". I had been thinking the same thing, so I rang Paul Merton, who I knew a bit. And Paul said, "Well, you've obviously got comic timing." I said, "Oh, thanks very much, thanks for noticing". He said "I'll put your name forward, but they're probably all booked". And that was it, bang. A few days afterwards, Hat Trick Productions rang and said they thought it was a wonderful idea and more or less wrote the show around me. I found them such a wonderful team to work with and it proved such a wonderful success for me. It was amazing the way it happened. That was the first time I've hustled. People have always come to me. But people weren't coming to me any more. Oh, no, there was none of that. That was the first time I've tried to get a job.'

And so the veteran of variety made his entrance into the bear pit that is *Have I Got News For You*. And what an entrance it was. Bruce bounded on through a glittery entrance, done up as if it were a game show, and started his banter with the audience. 'Welcome to *Have I Got News For You*. For you, have I got...' 'News!' the ecstatic

audience roared. Bruce next introduced the 'couples':
Paul Merton and Natasha Kaplinsky, and Ian Hislop and
Marcus Brigstock. Ian looked utterly bemused, an expres-
sion he was to retain throughout the show, which itself
was getting steadily more raucous every step along the
way. 'I've wanted the show to be like this for years!' cried
Paul Merton. 'I'm having the time of my life here!'

It was a mark of Bruce's standing in the industry
that that particular edition of *Have I Got News For You*
was adapted to fit in around him. Round two was 'Play
Your Iraqi Cards Right'. 'You know what? I never saw
this show,' said Ian, necessitating Marcus Brigstock to
explain to him the rules. Supposedly, said Bruce, round-
ing off the game, there were weapons of mass destruc-
tion in Iraq. 'Still, it'd be nice to see them.' 'Nice!' The
cards themselves showed wanted Iraqi war criminals,
and were to be handed out to American soldiers. 'Higher
or lower?' asked Bruce. 'I don't think this programme
can get much lower,' Ian replied. A little bit later in the
show, there was a conveyor belt of objects, from which
the teams had to pick the odd one out. It was a riotous,
uproarious success, and it changed the tenor of Bruce's
career overnight.

Asked afterwards if he'd had any idea what this

appearance would do for his career, Bruce sounded as staggered as everyone else. 'I wouldn't have believed them,' he told one interviewer who asked him what he would have thought if he knew what the programme was to lead to. 'It was all due to *Have I Got News For You*. I was a guest presenter on the show in June 2003. A lot of people thought it was a silly thing for me to do. A lot of people told me not to do *Have I Got News For You*. "You're asking for trouble!" they said. I did wonder how they'd take to me myself. You've got an audience that likes edgy humour, you know, a bit satirical, have a go at everybody. But within five minutes, they were like a game-show audience. I had such fun with them. I was very nervous before I went on. The audience of that show loves satire, and humour that insults people, so I thought, "How are they going to react to me?"'

Ian Hislop was asked if they were laughing with him or at him. 'Oh, with him,' he said. 'The "Iraqi Play Your Cards Right" was a new low in terms of bad taste on television, and actually I'm not sure anyone else would have got away with it. But he knows how to make an audience laugh. And you know what it's like in Britain – at a certain age people just like you. What's the Alan Bennett quote? "If you can boil an egg when you're eighty, you're a na-

tional institution." By the end I thought it was a hoot.'
Paul Merton, who has a fascination with comedians from
the old school, loved every minute of it. 'On *Have I Got
News for You* when they talk about the Home Office I
can't move on fast enough,' he said. 'I like stories like the
goldfish that burns the house down. I was in my element
when Bruce Forsyth was guest presenter.'

Many have seemed ideal presenters of this show until
they actually sat in the chair, leading to more than a few
disasters. Had it not gelled, Bruce could easily have been
one of them. Merton continued to shudder about the 'car
crash' when Neil Kinnock presented, and about the sour-
ness between Edwina Currie and Derek Hatton. 'They
were not good friends,' he said. 'It was an awful atmosphere. Sometimes MPs come a cropper when they have a
reputation for wit in the house, but that humour doesn't
work so well on the show. Jerry Hayes's jokes bombed,
but he ploughed on.'

As for Bruce himself – as he put it, 'They got a
Christmas special out of it. At the BBC, suddenly a light
went on and they thought: "Oh, he can still do something".
Have I Got News For You changed everything. I proved
to myself that I could still do it. It was that one show
that changed the course of my career and I'm so grateful.

Something amazing happened, and from being shut out of television, the doors opened and stayed open.'

The whole scenario was so unlikely as to be almost risible, and yet it worked. Equally unlikely was the fact that Bruce and Paul were becoming friends, going on to meet again on Paul's other show, *Room 101*. 'Paul is fascinated by old comedians, and took me for a drink to ask me all about the ones I've known and studied,' said Bruce. 'We've been friends ever since.'

From that moment onwards, the offers of work started flowing back in. There was *Didn't He Do Well*, not a programme – as might be supposed from the title – about Bruce himself, but one in which modern contestants were asked to answer questions used in older television contest shows. Bruce was everywhere, mingling with the new generation: he was even seen at the TV Quick Awards comforting a crying Craig from *Big Brother 6*.

But what had really changed was that he had by now gone beyond age, genre, and everything else by which British celebrities are defined. There was no longer any point in talking about the fact that he appealed to both young and old: he appealed to everyone. His very presence, while not always a guarantor of success, was still enough to bring in viewers on his own. He had seen it all, done it all, and was quite capable of doing it all over again, for Bruce had become timeless. Of course, he, and everyone else, was still conscious of his age, but the fact was that it simply didn't matter anymore. Bruce had transcended everything. He was Brucie, and while he might have had his detractors, his fans were far greater in number. He was loved as never before.

And so it was hardly surprising that the BBC, when it came up with its next great plan for Saturday night television, chose as one of its presenters the man who'd been showing the world how to do it for the best part of half a century.

Strictly Brucie

IT WAS IN 2004 that BBC bosses took a long, hard look at the schedules and thought about what they would do about the most important slot of the week. Saturday night used to tower over the rest of the week, but it was a good thirty years since the glory days of weekend television – when, as it so happened, one Bruce Forsyth used to dominate the proceedings. It was a difficult one to solve.

'For a long time, people have been asking, "What are we going to do on a Saturday night?"' said Wayne Garvey, head of the BBC's entertainment group. The answer was to return to what had worked before. For reasons that still mystify a lot of people, the BBC had axed *Come Dancing* several years previously – just, in fact, as a ballroom dancing phase started sweeping the country – and so, after some nail chewing, the decision was made to bring it back. But the added element this time would be that celebrities would be competing, and

the show would be called *Strictly Come Dancing*. And
who would be the ideal compere for the show? Step forward Bruce, along with his co-host Tess Daly. 'Jane Lush
[the BBC Controller] wrote me a letter after the ITV
thing and said she'd like to talk to me in the future,' said
Bruce. 'I wrote back saying I hadn't even thought about
more television. I just wanted a little period to relax and
feel what was going on.' Indeed, Bruce was clearly relish-
ing his most recent renaissance: two weeks before the
announcement that *Strictly Come Dancing* was to air,
he appeared on *Parkinson* on the BBC, the last one on
that channel before the venerable interviewer moved to
ITV. 'I was wondering who ITV were going to get to re-
place me – and you've got all that to look forward to,' he
crowed. 'Good luck!'

It was not his performance on *Have I Got News For
You* that put him forward for the role, but rather the fact
that he was ideal. Bruce was as popular as he ever had
been, a trained dancer himself, and second to none when
it came to hosting prime-time competition shows. He
was also able to think on his feet and was an absolute virtuoso at bringing in audiences. The irony was lost on no
one: the man who, twenty-five years previously, had been
declared to be past it by a new generation of 'alternative'

comedians was being hauled back in to save the day yet again. Of those alternatives, the vast majority had by now gone mainstream, and yet they still couldn't match Bruce. 'I've been forced to make another comeback!' he cried. 'It's better than going around with a begging bowl. It's wonderful to be back on television and I feel blessed to still be here.'

Bruce was clearly delighted. 'I love Saturday nights,' he said. 'The audiences are kinder, perhaps because they are drunk. It will be a family show,' he continued, and in truth, it was difficult to imagine him fronting anything else. 'Even children who only ever see dancing on *Top of the Pops* will like it. Older people who have been missing ballroom dancing on telly for the past ten years will love it. I mean, why oh why are we starved of Latin American music on the radio when the Brits love it? We're going out with all guns blazing.'

That family show element was important. This was to signal a return to the type of programme that everyone, young and old, could watch, and Bruce was the ultimate safe pair of hands. For all the ribaldry in his act, there was a line he wouldn't cross and that was essential for what was required now. 'I still don't like a lot of the dirty humour that's on at the moment,' he said. 'I have a yardstick. I grew up in the days when if there was a line in the script you'd say "Ooh, we'd better ask upstairs about that, it's a bit strong", and then they'd say, "No, you can't say that". And although I'm a lot cheekier now than I was forty years ago, I'm not downright dirty. It really is lavatory humour and, you know, sexual, where it's not even a double entendre. It's just dirtiness for the sake of it. I don't do that, and a lot of people respect that.'

Indeed, he brought an old-school ethos with him that was increasingly valued, and that included off stage as well as on. 'When you've been brought up in variety, I think timing is always important in your life,' he said. 'If I'm ever late for anything, whether it's personal or business, I always apologise. "I'm sorry I'm late", and all that. And if somebody is late meeting me, I expect them to say, "I'm sorry I'm late". It's just, shall we say, showbiz etiquette of my day.'

Bruce was also very excited about the format of the new show. 'Eight professional ballroom dancers will train celebrities in the waltz, quickstep, and Latin American,' he said. 'They'll be trained for six weeks, and the studio audience and a panel of judges will vote for the best progress. The celebrities are from all over the place: opera, soaps, a newsreader, and a rugby player. It's a lovely idea. I admire their courage. Of course, some of them were geed up at work to enlist.'

The contestants in the first series included Lesley Garrett, David Dickinson, Claire Sweeney, and Natasha Kaplinsky, whose own career soared once the show had aired. Others were *EastEnders* actor Chris Parker, rugby player Martin Offiah, Verona Joseph from *Holby City*, and the comedian Jason Wood. 'We have taken a legendary programme and given it a new twist for 2004,' Bruce went on. 'I was always a fan of *Come Dancing*. I loved to see the people getting up there, and the dancing was such a high standard. I think people won't know they've missed it until they see it. I love people talking back to me and me to them – and I'll be talking to the celebrities and judges after they've done their bit and I'm hoping I can have a bit of fun with them.'

Meanwhile, however, he had a few harsh words to say about the state that television was in. 'Those in charge pander too much to the young audience,' he said. 'There aren't that many younger presenters I can say that I like. But I do like Patrick Kielty. He's a good presenter, and a good stand-up comedian. I also like Jonathan Ross, although I'm not sure you'd call him young. I think he's marvellous. People such as Des O'Connor and Michael

Parkinson prove older presenters are still popular. I thought that I'd reached my sell-by date at sixty-five and it did go a bit quiet around that time. Then along came this big revival, which is marvellous at the grand old age of seventy-six.'

Bruce was, however, aware that he had detractors as well as fans. It didn't appear to bother him unduly. 'Yes, well, they're entitled to their opinion as long as they don't ruin your act,' he said. 'That's fine. I love when I'm doing my one-man show to see in the first few rows someone who is doubtful from the start. If they look like they're a little bit interested by the time you get to the interval, then that is wonderful. You've won them over.'

Bruce was now a combination of national treasure and institution, as he'd been around for so long. He didn't have to work: he wanted to, and his enthusiasm was hard to contain. 'I've made enough money not to have to work any more, but I enjoy it, I'm an entertainer,' he said. 'I can honestly say this last part of my life has been the best. There's no doubt about it. And that's down to my home life, my love life, and my career. I've been in the business so long because every generation has grown up with me since 1950 [sic] and they don't think of me as being particularly old. TV bosses forget that most people who watch the television are people post-forty or fifty. They're the people who stay at home in front of the box when the youngsters are out at a club. I'm looking forward to a new generation of kids and their parents watching me on Saturday nights and getting back to good old-fashioned family entertainment.'

The show was an immediate smash hit. The antics of the contestants garnered a good deal of attention, but at the same time, its incomparable compere was, deservedly, on the receiving end of a great deal of praise. 'It's a wonderful show,' he said. 'It's the hardest thing I've ever done, because I am not working to an audience. People are behind me, and at the side of me. I can't see them. But it's so good. It works for me, in spite of all the things about it that are against me. And people like me in it. Or they seem to.'

The BBC was equally delighted with the smash hit *Strictly Come Dancing* had become.

'Saturday nights haven't been this interesting for ten years,' said a delighted Wayne Garvie, head of the BBC entertainment group, as the show finished its first run. 'We have turned a big corner in BBC entertainment. We were a very difficult case two years ago; now we're in the midst of a very good period. We then went away, kicked it around in-house in the development team. If we were going to do something with celebrities, what would be a distinctive way for the BBC to do it? People thought we were a bit mad. We did a press launch and one journalist at the *Star* said we were barmy. Greg Dyke even took the piss out of me on *Have I Got News For You*. I thought there was something interesting about dancing. If we cast it properly, we'd achieve the slightly older BBC audience and bring in younger people, too. But I would be absolutely lying to you if any of us thought it would be quite as successful as it has been. But that's the genius of the team.'

It appeared that the most important member of the team was Bruce. 'He seemed like the most natural person to do it,' said Wayne. 'He's a phenomenon. A lot of people wince at Brucie's gags, but they've been wincing at them for forty-odd years and that's part of the charm. What I think is remarkable is that a man of his age can adapt to a modern entertainment show – a mix of reality, viewers voting, all live. He definitely brings in an audience that would not have watched the programme otherwise. And he can dance! I usually spend Thursday with Brucie, Natasha [Kaplinsky] or Tess [Daly], going through the script. It's a pleasure. Brucie was moaning the other day he had too much work. He goes to Costa Rica [sic] for holidays and he was worried about having to fit it in between the Christmas specials and his BAFTA tribute – we're running it on BBC1 in the New Year. Well, we're working on that. He's a very good roller skater.'

Strictly Come Dancing had the potential to make serious money for the BBC. It might not run advertisements, but it did sell formats, and after the success of *Strictly*, Wayne was cock-a-hoop. 'There's big money to be made but they're not necessarily rooted in British culture,' he said. 'We mustn't lose a sense of Britishness. That's where *Strictly Come Dancing* comes from. No other broadcaster was taking a risk by doing a ballroom dancing show. Two years ago, we completely restructured the entertainment department. It was failing. The stuff we were developing in-house wasn't good enough. We needed new blood so we recruited some new people and tried to create an atmosphere that people want to work in. The problem was, they thought all we did was *Big Break* and *The Generation Game*. They didn't want to come and join us to do twenty-seven weeks of the year. We started to do informal drinks with producers to show we weren't fusty, that we give people creative space to express themselves. That's why the department is working now. We're about four hundred people at peak, down to two hundred at others.'

There had been a little criticism from some quarters, but Bruce was able to acknowledge that. 'Of course I can read the autocue,' he said as he prepared for the second series to begin, this time to be co-presented with Natasha Kaplinsky. 'Yes, it was tough for the first series – we were feeling our way. There was a lot of work to get it right, and a lot of dashing about. This time round, we know the score and life will be a bit easier, though I'll be doing more singing and dancing slots. Those rumours about me packing it all in because I was exhausted were absolute rubbish. When you do a big live show like that it's bound to be tiring, but you keep going on the sheer excitement. There was never a moment when I felt so exhausted I thought I couldn't carry on. I tell you, when I walk on to the studio floor I feel thirty-seven, not seventy-seven. Something takes over. I've felt like that for the past forty years, although I must admit sometimes in the morning I do feel my age. It's entertainment, it's fashion, it's music, it's reality. The kids love it because they look at the screen and see people actually holding each other going round. That to them is like a human Playstation.'

Partly he managed to keep going because that famed

health routine was as rigorous as ever. 'I lead a safe life,' he said. 'I'm not a drinker. The most I'll have is one or two a week. And I don't overeat, but I make sure I have plenty of fruit and vegetables. I also make sure I get plenty of rest. If I've had a hard day I'll come in, lie down for a couple of hours, then get up for dinner. We always eat early, so my meal is digested properly. It's a performer's discipline, but it seems to pay off because people do marvel at me. I correct myself all the time, checking my posture when I'm driving or sitting down to eat or at a desk.'

The honours were now flowing in thick and fast. On 27 February 2005, the BBC screened *A BAFTA Tribute to Bruce Forsyth* to mark his sixty years in show business – almost six million viewers tuned in – while in May that year, a bust of Bruce, created by his son-in-law, was unveiled at the London Palladium. It stands in the Cinderella Bar.

In January 2006, it was announced that Bruce was to be awarded the CBE – Commander of the British Empire – a promotion from the OBE he'd been awarded in 1998. Even back then, though, there were mutterings that it should have been something much bigger than that: a knighthood. Other showbiz stalwarts had received them, and it was fair to say that no one, ever, had done more to entertain the nation than Bruce. *Strictly Come Dancing* had been re-commissioned again and it had also spawned an album, on which Bruce sang nine of the twenty-five tracks. 'My days of making albums were way, way gone, so many years I can't remember,' he mused. 'So to be given an opportunity to be in something like this, it's like being reborn.'

Certainly, the audience loved him. Why, Bruce was asked, is the older generation so popular on television? 'We haven't changed our styles,' he replied. 'People have grown up with us. All the programmes I've done have been for a family audience, so children have grown up with me for the last fifty years. I don't have to change my style to get an audience. But I'm still a person living in the twenty-first century; I try to keep abreast of the times. People have grown up with me since 1958. Every generation has grown up with me. And even the ones who hated me are still aware of me! And that's given me the durability that maybe a lot of other people haven't had. Retirement is always at the back of my mind. I think I'll know when is the right time to stop. When I walk on to a studio floor, I still feel as though I'm thirty-five. But there'll be one night when I walk onto the studio floor, trip over, fall on my face, and the first aid man comes. That'll be, "Thank you and goodnight!"'

The success of *Strictly Come Dancing* led Bruce to re-visit past triumphs, too. UKTV Gold was prompted to put on *The Generation Game: Now and Then*, showing some classic moments from the two sets of games Bruce hosted – in the 1970s and then again in the 1990s – prompting a flood of nostalgia from all concerned. 'We actually did get a grandfather who came back and was sitting there with his grandchildren who'd never seen him on screen. He'd said he was on television and the kids didn't believe him! There was one, Maureen, who lost her teeth and had this terrible laugh. When I met her again, she was exactly the same. You can't believe people are like this. I had to throw her off the stage whenever it was, 1975 or whatever, because she was laughing and we couldn't get on with the show.'

By this time, Bruce's show business awards were al-most too many to count. He had, amongst much else, won the Variety Club Show Business Personality of the Year in 1975, *TV Times* Male Personality of the year in 1957, 1976, 1977, and 1978, and BBC TV Personality of the Year in 1991. He twice has been voted the Greatest UK Game Show Host and in December 2007, 'Nice to see you, to see you, nice,' was voted the most popular UK catchphrase.

But Bruce can't last forever. As he turned eighty, one interviewer asked if he felt like the last of his generation: 'Oh, shut up! Shut up! How many floors up are we here, because I'm liable to open the window and jump out!' cried Bruce, but he conceded she was right. 'There's still Ronnie Corbett, bless his heart, and Jimmy Tarbuck, though he is about fifteen years younger than me. No, it is strange. I miss dinner with Frankie, and Les Dawson was such a darling. Tommy Cooper. The laughs you could have with Tommy! They will always seem the best years of my career because of the friendship. It's frightening, the way life speeds up. When you're at school, time can't go fast enough. But the last twenty-five years have been a blur. It's impossible to think that my wife and I have been together for twenty-five years. I have a son that she produced for me – she was determined to give me a son because I had five daughters before that – and he's twenty-one now.'

Alongside his career, Bruce's marriage to Wilnelia has gone from strength to strength. He has often been asked what keeps them together. 'We are great friends and we flirt with each other,' said Bruce. 'And she's the one who falls asleep on the sofa before me most nights. We laugh at the same things and we give each other space. If she wants to go off and do something, I say, "Okay, darling, have a lovely time," and she does the same for me. That's not to say that we live separate lives, just that we don't crowd each other.'

Asked what has been the secret of his success, Bruce was blunt. 'The secret was being lucky enough to get the job at the Palladium in the first place,' he said. 'In show business you can be the most talented person in the world, but you can also be the unluckiest and not get the right break at the right time. I was thirty years old when I got this break and it was absolutely wonderful for me. I think it always helped that I've been adaptable, that I do so many things – tap dance, play the piano, do impressions. There's also been a lot of hard work involved.'

A great deal has been written about Bruce over the years, but the fact is that his career has been an extraordinary one. He has surfed the wave of audiences moving from variety on live stage to its equivalent on television, has survived career setbacks and falling out of fashion – he's always fallen back in again – and has had career mishaps that would have floored a lesser man. And while he is undoubtedly talented, so are many other entertainers who don't have anything like the career he's had. Just how has he done it?

'Alfred Marks once said to me, "If I said what you say to people, someone would turn round and give me a clip round the ear. How do you do it?" I said, "I don't know, I just do it with a sense of humour and they accept it from me",' said Bruce. But it's more than that. Perhaps they recognise in Bruce a certain solidarity. After all, he came from humble beginnings and fought his way to the top. His material rewards have been great, but they've been fully earned. No one ever handed him anything on a plate.

Perhaps above all, though, Bruce represents a Britain that is almost now lost. He was born before World War Two, and came into his prime in the 1940s, an era of rationing and deprivation, certainly, but also one in which the country had a firm national identity. So much of it has been lost since then. Bruce represents a different era all together from the one that exists now, one that embodied innocent family entertainment. The alternative comedians might have lampooned him, but the fact remains that he is far more in touch with the man on the street than they ever could have been.

Bruce has nothing left to prove, no need to earn any

more money: he has become one of the show business greats. And, unlike so many, he's grateful for it, too. Of stopping, he said, 'I try not to think of it, but it's always in the back of your mind. At certain times of the day, you think, "How long will I be able to do all this?" It's giving me so much pleasure at the moment. No matter what happens, the fact that this opportunity has come along at this stage of my life means that ending doesn't worry me so much. I've been able to prove something before turning it in.'

He has certainly done that. There is only one more achievement that awaits him, one more honour to be sought after. How long, then, before it will finally be: Arise, Sir Bruce?